THE
Goddess
GUIDE TO
Divorce

The Goddess Guide to Divorce

A Memoir

By
Evelyne Michaut

AKASHA PRESS

Copyright © 2019 by Evelyne Michaut

All rights reserved. No part of this publication may be reproduced, distributed, or transmitted in any form or by any means, including photocopying, recording, digital scanning, or other electronic or mechanical methods, without the prior written permission of the publisher, except in the case of brief quotations embodied in critical reviews and certain other noncommercial uses permitted by copyright law.

For permission requests, please address akasha press at:
akashapress@gmail.com

Published 2019

ISBN: 978-1-64704-019-2

Library of Congress Control Number: 2019900140

Editing by Miranda Culp
Book design by Stacey Aaronson

Printed in the United States of America

To Claude and Patrick.
Thank you for making me who I am.

Contents

CHAPTER 1	Les Charmilles	/ 1
CHAPTER 2	Boogie Woogie	/ 9
CHAPTER 3	Death Tears Us Apart	/ 17
CHAPTER 4	Husband #1	/ 25
CHAPTER 5	Morass	/ 43
CHAPTER 6	Husband #2	/ 49
CHAPTER 7	Pain and Pleasure in LaLa Land	/ 63
CHAPTER 8	Hello Again, Divorce!	/ 81
CHAPTER 9	I Love You So Much . . .	/ 89
CHAPTER 10	The Prince	/ 99
CHAPTER 11	Husband #3: Third Time's the Charm	/ 109
CHAPTER 12	Marriage and Children	/ 113
CHAPTER 13	Constipation	/ 123
CHAPTER 14	Penis	/ 129
CHAPTER 15	Realizations	/ 133
CHAPTER 16	Healing	/ 143
CHAPTER 17	The Prince's Shadow	/ 153
CHAPTER 18	The Last Divorce	/ 165
CHAPTER 19	A New Chapter	/ 171

CHAPTER ONE
Les Charmilles

I can make it in fifty-seven seconds. If I run as fast as my little legs can take me. I am seven? Eight? Nine? I start counting the instant I close the front yard gate. One, two . . . reach the corner of our house . . . three, four, five . . . the manor's gravel alley is a blur . . . past my best friend Claire's house, the syncopated beats of my breath and heart overpower the street noises—I'm at the crossroad, don't stop for cars, the stately gate of the Charmilles across is target locked.

I'm now too big to run under the landscaped bushes so I go around . . . around . . . and bam! I'm at the gate of the south wing, at my grandparents' yard. I jump over, run up the steps, and ding-dong! Beat my own record again, maybe . . . the counting is free-form. Usually Bon-Papa opens. Always in a suit. He takes a bath every morning, my dad has said with some awe. My grandpa is: Brains. Discipline. Difficult. But he can be sweet. Always smiling. Four kisses on the cheeks. We visit. If it's coffee time, I'm allowed to dunk a cube of sugar in his cup. Coffee-flavored sugar melting on my tongue. Bonne-Maman asks me every five minutes if I have a boyfriend. Bon-Papa objects: "She needs to study!" and I let them do their little thing—they have been together what, fifty? Sixty years?

I may wander through the clinic. Go through the tall wooden doors to the main building. Past the utility stairs that lead to the basement where my father has an office tucked between the huge storage rooms, fridges, kitchens. Past the administration where *les petites dames du bureau,* the little office ladies, are crammed amidst filing cabinets and large typewriters. I could walk in and say hi to Aunt Bathilde. She's got Bonne-Maman's big round office now, but I'd have to walk through the cloud of perfumes, hair spray, and chit-chat. Besides, my aunt scares me a little. I go straight through the next set of double doors and into the entrance hall. I love standing in the middle and looking up to the first-floor mezzanine and the high ceilings. This? A humble hunting retreat for Napoleon III? Built when this area just fifteen kilometers southeast of Paris was open fields. I try to imagine it without the hospital smell of antiseptic attempting to cover up infected wounds and incontinent people. Blur out the handicapped ramps and doors, the linoleum. The grand ballroom partitioned into physical therapy booths.

One modern addition I love is the vending machine tucked under the grand staircase. If I've got change, I get myself a Coca-Cola bottle, and then ride the tiny cage elevator. I have nightmares for years about that rattly thing taking me to weird nonexistent floors on the way up, or not stopping on the way down.

The patients here are mostly old. They fell at home and broke a hip, or they have "diabetes" and so their foot had to be cut off. Sometimes there's a younger guy missing half a leg (motorcycle accident, almost always). When the Arab sheikh who drove over a land mine came, they gave him an entire floor for his retinue. Once, I even saw a little girl in a wheelchair, one leg entirely absent from the hip bone. Maman explained that her mama had put a knitting needle inside her belly when the baby was in it, to try to get it out. But it didn't work; it just scraped off the leg. "Bon-Papa will fix it," she promised. The clinic makes prosthetic limbs that are fitted exactly to the patient, and then they teach you to walk with it.

 I take the elevator to the fourth floor. It's under the roof so the ceilings are lower, and it makes for a cozier room for the patients. But few people ever hang out here. Empty tables with board games, a couple of patients in wheelchairs, a beat-up grand piano out of tune. The best here is the giant exterior clock. You can go behind it! There is only the frosted glass and the reverse Roman numerals of the dial between me and the park, forty feet below. My dad showed me because sometimes he goes himself to wind up the clock mechanism with the big key. Loud tick-tock, though really it doesn't work well, and I don't think anyone in the park ever looks at it for the time.

 Down the utility stairs to the first floor where I switch to the rarely used grand staircase, just for the pleasure of strutting down the wide white steps that curve to the main hall. Left at the bottom toward the sixties' addition, past the receptionist—I know she can see my little head but I dash toward the gymnasium. There's usually no one here after lunch and I am free to goof on the stationary bikes, giant bouncy balls, asymmetrical bars, and the terrifying high platform with hole and fireman's pole. Bon-Papa was an Olympic gymnast and a fireman before going to medical school and starting the pioneering clinic that earned him the Legion of Honor.

 I am having fun at the gym (I think!). I want to dare. I want to be dared. Look what I can do! I can do it! I can jump from on high, I can climb all the way up the ladders though my legs shake. I am an acrobat—my body will do what I will it to do.

 Is there room for softness? I don't remember. Maman is soft. Does she hug me? One breast is soft. One is bouncy because it's silicon. I like to jiggle it when she leaves it in the bathroom closet. I like her perfumes too. Diorissimo . . . floral notes of lily of the valley transport me to her. Toward the end she bought Dior's Poison. Dark purple bottle. Toward the end. There was an end. It was coming and I knew it. Dark purple bottle of death. Too strong, my dad said. Too womanly.

The gymnasium opens to the park, toward the pond. I wander outside. I'm glad for the low wire fence that keeps the swans in. Sometimes I tease them, and they run at me wings open, neck extended, quacking angrily, the males especially. I get to the top of the Grande Allée, straight view to the stone urn at the bottom of the park. I love running down because of the slope—makes me feel like I'm flying. This is where I learned to bike. My dad just pushed me at the top and . . . off I went! In the fall I collect the spikey pods and smooth brown chestnuts that the trees drop all over. I try to avoid being seen. People on crutches and wheelchairs make me uneasy, especially when they don't wear their prosthetics. Sometimes they don't even cover their stumps and you can see the puffy purple-red scars where the limb ends and the skin has been tucked in. Most of the employees know me and want to say hello. I am embarrassed. They may introduce me to their colleague. "*C'est la petite fille du Docteur Michaut.*" I am someone. I am the granddaughter of Doctor Michaut. And everyone knows who that is. He's the big boss. He started it, after all. I get the feeling he's a bit of a Napoleon, running this place with an iron fist. At least until recently. I feel I own the place, a little bit. I belong here. But maybe not everyone feels that way. Maybe they resent the fact that his wife was the administrative director, and now his elder daughter. His son directs the custom prosthetics department. Maman works here too, of course. My dad. Cousins at times. I will work here too, later.

For now this is my world. This is where we all gather: Maman, her sister Bathilde—we call her Bab, and little brother Robert—we call him Bob. And the spouses and the cousins. I am comfortable only with my grandpa and grandma, and cousin Emilion. Bab's girls are older. Bab herself is never quite there. She is always behind a cloud of smoke. She smokes Dunhill, red, only halfway, and puts them in the gold standup ashtray that stays near her Louis XIV brocade armchair by the grand piano. She constantly nurses a whiskey-coca, ample hair piled in a messy nest on top of her head, legs tucked under her. Bob always has the same inane jokes. I avoid him. I don't think they care for me. I am invisible. Do they even know who I am? Can they see me?

I only like cousin Emilion. He is my age and he is real. He sees me and we play together. He is fun and he is game. Together we climb the big branch that bends far over the pond—how far can we go above the mean swans who pinch you with their nasty beaks if they catch you?

One Christmas Eve it is so cold, the pond is frozen and though it is dark, we are sliding on the ice in our dress-up shoes. When we are sick of being outside, we tear through our grandparents' apartment. Go down the scary stairs to the basement. I have nightmares for years about turning the corner. It is dark and shape-shifting and there are things there, people, hiding in the pantry or the spare room. But with Emilion we can go anywhere. We hide in the storage room and we might show each other what the other doesn't have, quickly pulling pants down then up, choking on our own giggles. Then the adults call us. "Kids! Kids! You just missed Santa!" What? It's already midnight and we missed Santa? Again? Again? Quickly, we run up the stairs through the entrance down the hallway into the grand salon. The maid has cleaned up the twenty-five place settings with the help of cousins. The extended table we'd been playing under while grownups overate smoked salmon and boudin blanc and goose is back to its normal size and we can see, at the foot of the big tree, a mountain of gifts. Forget Santa! Let's open the gifts! Oh no—first, Maman is going to sing "*Minuit Chrétiens*" while aunt Bathilde accompanies her.

We sit under the piano. I love her voice. I can feel her voice and the piano strings vibrating through my little rib cage. *Peuple . . . à genoux!* She says, imperative, "People . . . kneel! Expect your deliverance! Here comes your Redemptor!" I can feel her heart. Everybody else says Jesus is bullshit but the way she sings that, I know he is not.

The family claps, Bon-Papa criticizes his daughters for too much use of the pedal and not bridging those two notes quite right, and then it's a mad dash to the tree. Kids who can read distributing presents as fast as they can, wrapping paper flying, oohs and aahs and laughter and thank-yous and kids sorting the good gifts (a Barbie doll!) from the disappointing ones (a book).

An uncle puts a record on, something American, rock 'n' roll, and the cousins swing barefoot on the Aubusson rug.

Patrick is bored. He is in a chair in the hallway reading *Time* magazine. The family thinks he's rude because he doesn't partake. But already I can see why—it's the same conversations every year. Every gathering. Same thing. There is love. But there is something broken too. There are hushed things. We don't talk about Bathilde's grief (cousin Yannick, her fourth child, her only boy, was two when he drowned—it's only been five, six, seven, ten years). I think I caught a whisper about my mom. "Doctor so and so said . . ." Frowns, sighs.

But kids at these gatherings get a super treat: we can sit in Bon-Papa's office downstairs, leather couch and custom bookshelves filled with classic volumes, with a space in the middle for the TV and VCR, and watch the one VHS tape of two hours of Tex Avery cartoons. "Much better than Walt Disney," say the grownups with knowing nods. We love Droopy and Bugs Bunny and Daffy Duck and Woody Woodpecker and, especially, the unpronounceable Screwy Squirrel. Some of their lines are used year round in our house.

It's two a.m.—things are quieting in the living room. Bon-Papa wheels in his crêpe cart—he's making crêpes suzette, thinly sliced oranges and Grand Marnier for flambé. Blue flames, right in the living room. We're not hungry but they taste so good. Tomorrow—or today, actually—we will sleep in and lounge around our own house up the street, recovering.

One hot summer day, bumming around our backyard, I have this idea that I need something in the cave. I open the creaky, peeling wooden door and there, on the fourth stone step, Maman is sitting. Something is not right. Her face is swollen. Weight on my chest. "Maman!" I cry out, "*Qu'est ce que tu fais là?*"

"*J'ai chaud, pitchounette.*" I'm hot, little one. I am her little one. She loves me, that word says. But she is sorry that I found her here. I can tell. She's just hot, she says. Yeah, that makes sense. It's a sweltering day and the cave is cool, the three-foot-thick stone wall, the darkness. Her husband is with her friend Chantal, somewhere upstairs. The cancer has taken over. Her body, swollen and deformed by drugs, treatments. The shapeless purple dress that she tries to hide under. The wig. Still she wears makeup, and perfume. Is she feminine, my maman? Is she crying because she is alone? Where is her family? Nobody comes to visit.

Oh yes, sometimes a younger cousin. They love my dad. They think he is so funny, so charming. Do they know? Does she ever complain? Say anything? Ask for help? She receives everyone with love. Opens her arms, smiles, laughs her high-pitched laughter. When she drinks wine, her cheeks turn bright red.

One evening I am setting the dinner table and Patrick tells me not to put the bottle of red on the table. He says she shouldn't drink. When she sits, she gets mad. There are tears in her eyes. Something is going on that I don't understand. It is close to the end.

"That's the one thing, the one thing, that I get to do. I can drink if I want to, *merde!*"

She stands.

She said *merde*.

Shit.

She grabs the car keys, slams the garage door. Patrick follows her.

"Leave me ALONE!" she yells while rolling open the garage door. Gets in the blue Peugeot. Slams the door. Takes off. Patrick and I are left bereft. He seems so . . . disarmed. So sad. Like he fucked up. Like he really cares. Like, she makes a good point. What is the point of her not drinking a little wine at dinner?

What is the point.

CHAPTER TWO

Boogie Woogie

"Pa-neeeek!" yells my dad. He's acting berserk, it's hilarious and we all get excited, including the dogs who start running in circles and knocking me over.

All hands on deck: guests are coming.

It's a rather rare occurrence. One that warrants a massive sweep of the construction dust, ashes from the large open fire, dog hairs, clothes tools books toys covering all surfaces. We usually live nonjudgmentally amidst the chaos, though it is fun to rally the troops—me, older sister Nina, Maman, Dad, and the dogs—for a once-over, once in a while, and do a little justice to the old house.

In the mid '70s my parents bought the derelict nineteenth-century house up the street from Les Charmilles. My dad, a gifted do-it-yourself guy, fixed it up with his hands and the sweat of his whole body. We lived in dust and demolition debris often, in what he called a state of "temporary permanence," the house forever unfinished. For as long as I can remember I loved working with my dad, even though I got occasionally yelled at for not finding the right tool in the scary pile of stuff in the basement.

There were always animals in and around the house. Always: dogs, who ran the house and whose hair would coalesce into giant dust bunnies that drove my mother nuts. Most of the time: cats, who met various dismal fates. I found one flattened near the fountain—he'd lost in the chase with Ollen the boxer mutt, unable to reach the safety of the six-foot perimeter wall. Another one died from eating meat my mom had forgotten on the counter to defrost. Kittens born in the straw bale shed met the back of my dad's shovel.

At random times we had ducklings that my dad was raising for the large pond in the clinic's park, so they wouldn't be eaten by rats. Catching and squeezing ducklings was good sport, and a delight—they are so soft and squishy. Until they poop on you. There were idiotic dwarf hens who couldn't remember to keep their eggs warm. My dad organized a "survival mission" where we "hunted" in the backyard, caught, killed, and plucked. That was that for the chickens episode.

Then there were the maimed animals that people would bring us to rescue, though our success rate was low. The lost turtle, Sidonie, made it the longest. The limping hedgehog fell into a bucket of old motor oil. The cute little bat survived after hanging off the cornice of the antique kitchen hutch for a week. My mom, who collected owls, was excited when someone brought us a real baby one. She set it up in the spacious downstairs bathroom, but we didn't know to feed it whole animals, so she was sickly and ended up drowning in the toilet bowl. Nina and I were of course blamed for leaving the lid up.

My favorite was Leon. Leon the crow. My dad had come up with the name because his raucous cry sounded a bit like that: Leeeh-on! Someone brought him to our house because he was, according to them, "too friendly." Leon had been dancing in front of the bus, possibly with a broken wing, preventing the poor driver from driving away. He healed, but adopted us and hung out for a whole summer. Leon loved to sit on my mom's shoulder and rub his head lovingly on her cheek. He stole cherries from the fruit bowl and stuffed them in the wicker of the kitchen chairs for later consumption—but forgot until we found them rotted. He hated red nail polish and would launch himself, wings spread with an offended cackle, at Chantal's painted toes. Once he flew to the old couple's kitchen in the manor next door and picked at the camembert they'd left on the table. Eventually he disappeared. We heard reports of women's toes being attacked at the bus stop a couple times, and then nothing. His closeness to humans probably did him in.

Claire lived in the house on the other side of the manor. We were a year and a half apart and inseparable. To get to her house I would climb the tree nearest the backyard wall, jump down the other side and cross the manor's alley, clamber over Claire's stonewall, and voilà, we would meet at the back of her garden and create our secret world together.

One day, my sister and I were awakened early by my dad's booming voice. What trouble are we in now? We rush down the stairs. I'm six years old but I'm already super good at taking them four by four. I am a superhero gliding down the two flights at top speed, always just a little scared I'm not going to land right on that fourth step and break my neck.

"Girls!" the big voice said (I'm not sure if it is angry). "Downstairs! Now!"

I find Patrick outside the kitchen. Patrick is our dad. He doesn't like for us to call him papa—papa is for old farts. He is young and cool so we call him Patrick. Sometimes Pat.

On the grass, beside my father with his trademark crooked smirk, is . . . a pony.

First, I feel relieved. We are not in trouble! But then I'm kind of puzzled. Why is this giant creature munching on the grass in front of the kitchen. It's looking a little twitchy, and not very cuddly.

Patrick is standing proudly in front of the brown and white

Pinto. Patrick is tall, muscular, his soft brown hair always a bit messy. And he smells strongly of "man," an odor that goes away briefly on Sundays when he showers.

"He's an Irish Connemara," he says in his "I know stuff" voice, like it's supposed to mean anything to us. "Not a ridiculous pot-bellied dwarf thing."

"A beautiful little horse," he insists.

It's true. Even I can see that the pony's features are gracefully proportioned.

"And," the smirk comes right back, "I certainly am not going to have him gelded. This guy is staying whole!"

I knew what that meant because I was familiar with the twice-a-year nonsense of keeping Ollen locked in the basement for two weeks while the bitches were dripping blood around the house. We'd failed to do that when we first adopted him because he was only a few months old, and he'd managed to impregnate the ten-year-old female, making my dad very proud.

So I learned to ride on seven hundred kilos of youth, muscle, and testosterone.

We called the pony Boogie-Woogie.

My dad set up an enclosure big enough for him to walk around at the back of the yard. The first few months, Boogie systematically destroyed every fence my dad put up. He'd just lean on it, crush it, and graze in the rest of the yard. Finally my dad found some enormous beams that had been used for railway tracks and built a Boogie-proof fence. He also added an electric wire, which I practiced grabbing as an occasional test to myself.

To let Boogie out of his enclosure, I'd have to unlatch the gate while he watched me intently, making snorting sounds and shaking his head wildly, then kick the gate open, mold myself for refuge to one of the beams, and let the crazed little stallion run out in an explosion of hoofs. After about ten minutes he'd settle, occasionally airing his penis that almost touched the grass when it was fully extended.

Boogie was very clever. He could open door handles with his deft, muscular lips. On occasion, we forgot about him grazing in the yard. He'd get bored after a couple hours and suddenly he'd be in the dining room with us.

When he was in his enclosure, I would go visit Boogie by jumping over the fence. He was rough at times, not a cuddly pony. I never felt he particularly cared for me. And he was a lot of responsibility. I resented having to feed him three times a day —the path to the back of the yard seemed so long, and we had to do it in all weather. We had to shovel his poop too. And though I'm sure my dad did most of the caretaking, I always felt I had to do it more than my (lazy) older sister.

Still, Boogie and I had a kind of friendship. I loved brushing his hair and cleaning his hoofs and he would indulge me. I'd read in a book that horses greet by sniffing each other's noses. So I'd taken to doing that with him. I could fit half my face in his nostril and we'd sniff loudly at each other for a bit. After that he'd let me pat and brush him.

But to get to him, I first had to get past Margot.

Margot was the goat destined for the slaughterhouse that we'd rescued on a trip to Chantal's dad's farm in the country somewhere. Such a tiny, cute, soft white thing, with an irresistible baby bleat and milky breath. My mom fed her with a bottle. We knew Boogie needed a buddy so we took Margot home. They became besties in an odd couple kind of way.

But Margot grew, and grew, and her horns grew, and grew. There was no question of trimming them; it seemed as cruel as castrating a dog. Her head was as high as mine. She towered when she got on her hind legs.

I want to get to Boogie. So I jump the fence. But there is

Margot, planted on her four legs, staring straight at me. She charges, head down and cocked to the side. But I know what to do: I camp myself firmly on the ground and let her get close . . . then swiftly grab a horn in each hand.

And I hang on.

She shakes and shakes her head wildly, and I hang on. I can see she's getting pissed off. She can't rise on her hind legs, she can't butt me. Eventually, she gets tired of shaking my little weight around with her head and quits. She lets me through and doesn't bother me after that. My heart is racing but I go sniff Boogie's nose.

Then, there was the actual riding. For that, Patrick bought a long practice lead. He'd take us to the manor because there was a large park. Dede would wheel her hemiplegic husband onto the balcony—I would wave and see him light up. I liked going there because I knew they got so much joy out of watching us. Also their park was easier to ride in because it was walled, and because they'd sold half of it to the town to turn into a public park, the size was manageable. I was much more scared of riding in the clinic's park. Les Charmilles was surrounded by seven acres of not-so-landscaped open grass and woods. Not to mention the risk of running into amputees taking a stroll.

We'd practice with the lead for a bit, learning commands and terms. Boogie tolerated me on his back. He'd been sufficiently trained to respond to hand and leg. He was reasonably willing to practice *volte* and *demi-volte*, trot and canter. Then my dad would unclip the lead from the bridle and walk alongside me, or sometimes jog, through the park. Or call out commands from the center of the field.

Every so often, especially when I was littler, lighter, and a beginning rider, Boogie would take off. Maybe he was sick of being obedient to the shrimp on his back. Sometimes he'd pretend to be scared off a bush. He'd just bolt, and there was nothing for me to do but grab a handful of mane and hang on.

It's happening again. I tell myself it's okay because daddy is running behind holding the lead. But when I peek back, the lead is dragging on the ground and Dad is far behind with his hands up in the air.

I know he trusts me to hang on. He uses big words when he talks about me, like "pugnacious" and "tenacious." They sound like good things. I can prove to him that I'm strong and make him proud. I'm hanging on. Grass is a blur. Trees are a blur. I simply will not fall. I've fallen once into the patch of stinging nettles at the bottom of the field and I am not doing that again.

Boogie is galloping full speed now. I have a feeling he is enjoying this. As for me, I'm not sure what is more thrilling: the speed, or my own determination to hang on in spite of his efforts to dismount me.

He's headed for the woods. I know that he knows that that's the scariest for me. He must be really pissed off today. The trick he likes to play on me is to head straight for a trunk, full gallop, and at the last second do a nimble sideways jump.

This time, I see the big chestnut coming at me. I feel Boogie do his fast sidestep under me but . . . I must have lost my grip. I keep going straight. I feel my body wrap itself around the trunk. My chest empties in one loud *oomph*. I feel myself slide to the base of the trunk.

I regain consciousness in the grand bedroom of the manor. I don't remember, but apparently I've walked up here. The old couple is looking at me with concern. My dad sports his amused-proud smirk. "She's a tough one, hey?" Mind over matter—the motto my dad repeats often to me, in English, pops into my head.

I laugh too—that was pretty funny.

Straight out of a Tex Avery cartoon.

CHAPTER THREE
Death Tears Us Apart

Tuesday, April 15th, 1986. I am a twelve-year-old middle-schooler waiting on the curb to be picked up. The blue Peugeot turns the corner. But instead of Maman in her fur coat at the wheel, it's my dad, as it has been for the last week.

"Did you go to the hospital today?"

"Yes."

"How is she?"

Silence.

He is looking at the road.

"*Tu sais, ta maman . . . c'est fini.*"

Finished.

Maman.

A week ago she drove us to our piano lesson in Paris. Afterwards, as usual, we went to Aunt Bathilde's. Nina and I went straight into the living room. Someone popped the tape of *My Fair Lady* into the VCR, but Maman turned left to go to the bedroom.

We never saw her again.

We didn't see the ambulance that came for her. Later, we were told she was in a coma.

They didn't take us to the hospital. "She wouldn't have wanted you to see her that way."

That way.
What way?
I would have liked to see her.

※

WEDNESDAY APRIL 16TH, 1986.

Breakfast. Patrick says:

"I jumped awake at 5:20, felt your mother's presence. Then at 5:30 I got a call from the hospital. 'Monsieur? Your wife passed away ten minutes ago.'"

8:30 a.m. I am at school, in line with my classmates to enter history class. The principal, terrifying Monsieur Vignes, is overseeing the hallways. He comes to me, bends, asks softly: "*Et comment va ta maman?*"—how is my mom? Tears explode from my eyes. I blurt out: "*Elle est morte ce matin.*"

She died. This morning.

※

BLURRY IMAGES OF the stairs to the morgue, grownup lower bodies crowding us. One clear image through the door to the room where her body lies in an elevated coffin: a chestnut curl of her hair poking out above the edge of the coffin. I walk toward the door but a grownup grabs me, holds me back. "No!" she exclaims. "They shouldn't see her that way!"

※

IS THIS A CHURCH? A giant, light-filled hall. Someone talking on a podium. Someone asks, "Who will walk to the cremation chamber?"

"I will," I say. I remember thinking it might be interesting.

Me and my dad. We walk beside the coffin, enter an elevator, descend. I watch as the coffin is put on rollers like a suitcase at the airport. A mechanical jaw slides up—there are flames in there. The coffin is swallowed.

We wait.

We are handed an urn.

It is warm.

SOME WEEKS LATER, my dad, my sister, and I, in Brittany, standing on the promontory known as La Pointe du Raz, furious Atlantic waves smashing into the rocks. This is where we spent our last vacation as a family—just Maman, Papa, sister, and me. She loved this place. She wanted her ashes thrown to the *quatre vents*—to the four winds. We put our hands in the urn. The ashes feel soft, but there are gritty little bones too. I open my hand and the wind takes it all away. And just like that, she is one with the ocean.

SOME MONTHS LATER, Nina and I take turns babysitting. Today it's me. I don't know where Chantal is. Chantal, it turns out, now lives permanently with us. She had been Maman's close friend. She used to stay weekly in the guest room. It's 1986—women wear shoulder pads, and we dance to pop singer Jean-Jacques Goldman's hit *"Elle a fait un bebe toute seule"* (she had a baby by herself). Nina and I think it's hilarious that the song talks exactly about what our family friend is doing.

Chantal was seven months pregnant when Maman died. She did not attend the funeral. Now I've got baby Ronan in the carriage, and when I tried going up the steps to the kitchen, he almost fell out. Tiny little thing—I got so scared! For him, and also because Chantal screams a lot.

⚭

MAMAN HAS BEEN gone over a year. We don't talk about her. We removed her photos so as not to confuse "the little boy." Baby Ronan is sitting in the high chair. His mom is trying to feed him but he is crying. She grabs him by the arms and shakes, shakes him. Her face is bright red. "I will squish you!" she screams. I watch as his little head, face bright red too, goes back and forth, back and forth, fast. I hate her. I do not understand. I thought she wanted a baby so bad.

⚭

TWO YEARS LATER:

"Girls . . . ?"

The honey voice is coming from the second floor. What does she want now? My sister and I come down from our rooms.

Chantal is in the doorway of my mom and dad's room—oh right, it's hers and my dad's room—holding Maman's fur coat. Nina and I stand a couple steps up from the landing, waiting.

"So I was thinking . . . do either of you, I mean do you envision ever wearing Claude's mink coat? Because, you know, it's kind of old fashioned and you too are teenagers, and this is a woman's coat."

We stare at her in our practiced neutral stance. Never know where the land mines are. She forges ahead:

"So anyway, I was thinking, instead of it staying unused in a closet . . . it would be such a waste . . . if you don't have any objection, I could have it recut to fit me. You don't have any objections, do you?"

There it is, that familiar hard thing in my chest. It rolls down like an iron curtain. I'm scanning with my mind for any reason she shouldn't do this. I can't come up with any. I mean, she's right, I'm not going to use Maman's fur coat. It's just a coat, and anyway, who cares. Same for the rings that were resized for Chantal's small fingers. Did we see how delicate they are? And same goes for the stately dining table that was packed up and stored in the shed.

And the bed! Oh the bed—I have to roll over with laughter at that one. Gone the classic '70s designer bedroom set, and in with the . . . drumroll . . . black pleather waterbed! I'm dying. Complete with a wall of mirrors for a headboard.

So the coat, who cares.

"No of course, sure." I turn around to go back upstairs. I hear nothing from my sister. "Go for it," I add.

TURNS OUT, Les Charmilles and this odd little suburban town ain't what it seemed when I was a kid. Now I really see the projects across the street. I hang out there sometimes, with the black and Arab dropouts who sell hasheesh. They treat me with the kindness and good humor reserved for aliens. The conversations are boring as fuck, standing next to a scooter on the street talking about sneakers or some stupid shit someone did, but their made-up backward language sounds cool and it's a nice diversion from my house.

Any outing into Paris requires a tedious bus ride to a sordid metro station. Still, I'd do anything to get out, so I bum around Les Halles or the Île de la Cité with no money, longing for this other life everyone else is living. Everything is cold and gray. In the summer it's hot and gray. An occasional pastime on the long metro line into the city is to imagine myself in sudden crashes: trains, cars, buses, my body splattered and dismembered, and me, instantly free. Free of the idiocy of my stepmother, of the incessant yelling about inane domestic issues. What? My sister or I left our laundry for the maid to iron? What? You ate the crackers that were reserved for me and my son? My dad mulishly silent when she explodes at us, hands flying.

He basically vanished when she officially moved down one flight of stairs from the guest room into the master bedroom. Sometimes I can get into a good debate with him at dinner, about my philosophy class for instance, but Chantal slams the kitchen cupboards loudly until he pays attention to her.

We don't see much of Maman's family. Aunt Bathilde's daughters used to come for dinner sometimes with their husbands. But I don't feel close enough to my cousins to run some of these things by them. They seem to adore my dad, and Chantal is all honey when they visit. So I just sit through the dinners. Then they stop coming. Apparently Bathilde gave an ultimatum: "Step in that house one more time, and never speak to me again."

I can go across the street once a week to visit my grandparents, but I cannot talk about anything that goes on in my house. Bon-Papa will not hear the name of "that woman." Or my dad's.

I am fifteen, sixteen, seventeen. There is a lawsuit. Patrick and Chantal have taken sides with the people at the clinic who ousted my grandpa from the board, then fired Bob and Aunt Bathilde, who are suing for wrongful termination. I want to throw up every night at dinner as I'm forced to listen to them perseverate over all the ways in which my grandpa and aunt did wrong. I think: don't they remember they owe their job to these people?

(And: Do they forget who I am?)

I think the American TV series *Dallas* has nothing on us.

I sleep as much as I can through these years, then fuck off from that house at the first opportunity.

CHAPTER FOUR

Husband #1

I met husband #1 when I was nineteen.

I had saved money to go to America for the summer, a longtime dream of mine. I'd wanted to go to San Francisco, but my uncle had poo-pooed the idea, saying too many French people hung out there. He set me up instead with his old-time friend John, who lived on Long Island. I would take care of the kids along with another French girl, Stephanie, and do some odd jobs.

The house on Duck Pond Road was something out of the movies. A rambling Cape Cod–style complete with wraparound porch, peeling paint, and five cars. I got to drive the Jeep truck and the Jaguar—a nice change from my mom's old Peugeot. The kids were cute and not too much work since I shared duties with Fanny (a nickname we quit using on learning "fanny" had another meaning).

There was another guest in the house, but my English comprehension wasn't a hundred percent then and I didn't fully get what he was doing there. His bedroom was off the kitchen, not upstairs like ours. More to the point, he was 6'4", blue-eyed, with shoulders tanned and broad from building the fence. He was a "Kiwi." I had no idea where New Zealand was on the map, let alone what a Kiwi was, but I became very interested very fast.

I learned that Craig was "bumming around the world,"

which meant he was traveling on the cheap, staying at friends' friends' friends' places, earning money with occasional jobs. Ah! A globetrotter! An explorer! An adventurer! So worldly and so wise! (He was turning twenty-five.)

I'd always longed to escape my little Parisian suburb and to travel far and wide. Between that and the above-described suntan/shoulders/blue eyes, I was done for. It took three or four long weeks to find out, with utter surprise, that he too was interested in me. He winked at me while riding a merry-go-round at the fair. Since he was a pilot in New Zealand, he'd chosen to scrunch his long legs into the kiddy airplane, holding the tiny joystick and flashing his perfect teeth at every turn. That is how I learned the word "wink." John mumbled, "Huh, Craig winked at you." I had to ask what "wink" meant. When he showed me, I could deduct that the interest was mutual.

From wink to bed took a lot less time. One free afternoon we drove the open jeep to a semi-private beach. Craig was floating on an inflatable raft, avoiding the jellyfish, his tanned skin and blue eyes shimmering in the sun. I got in the water to join him. He hoisted me up on the tiny raft with his natural, gentle ease, flashing his perfect teeth. And we kissed.

I wasn't a virgin, having had a couple of mediocre teenage experiences. But I discovered hot sex that summer on Long Island. By then John had kicked Craig out of the house—he didn't want any nonsense with his French wards—so we would meet in a friend's basement where he was crashing. And it was hot. The summer heat, and our two young bodies going at it like I had never experienced. I don't remember orgasms, but excitement? A-plenty. Sex, sweat, skin sliding on skin, repeat. Smoking cigarettes in bed and eating cereal out of the box because we were starving but didn't want to leave the room.

Very soon after that, we were on a real airplane to backpack around the world together. Law studies be damned, I could always get back to university later, but I was NOT going to miss out on this love-and-world-tour adventure. I couldn't care less what Patrick would say. I was nineteen and legally, an adult!

I called him up. "I'm putting law school on hold for a year and going traveling with this guy from New Zealand."

"You'll never go back to university! And how are you even going to live?"

"I will too finish my degree! And Craig is buying the tickets and he's a very experienced traveler. We'll work our way through."

Besides, Aunt Kali (my dad's own sister!) helped me out with a check.

Seems so romantic, I know. I was completely infatuated, and enamored also by what I saw as the absolute originality of the story. For a girl growing up in a sad urban outskirt of Paris, what was the likelihood of meeting a New Zealander in New York and going backpacking in Asia?

We first flew to Christchurch, where Craig was from. We met his parents outside the little town of Geraldine. The air and everything so clean, so green. The wide main street lined with white wooden houses, and sweet stores with parking spots right in front of them. People greeting you, always, and with a smile! No traffic, ever.

His parents lived on a "station"—they couldn't call it a farm because it was so ginormous, something like 15,000 hectares of pastures. That's where Craig learned his hardy outdoor skills: driving all kinds of vehicles including twin-engine planes, herding cattle, fixing things. Diving into wild waterfalls.

Craig's mom made Pavlova cake for me with the local fresh cream and I felt loved in a way I hadn't experienced since . . . I couldn't remember.

From there we hitchhiked our way to the north of the country. Already, our relationship was settling into a routine. I was still in awe of Craig, but also learning quickly not to be so terrified of traveling. Turned out, people were pretty friendly and helpful on the backpacking trails. Striking up conversations and exchanging information pre-Google was very easy. I realized there is no such thing as traveling alone.

We made it to Sydney but didn't stay because it was too expensive. The trick for long-term backpackers is always to find the cheapest hostel and get away from the touristy (read: desirable) areas. Greyhound buses took us all the way up the eastern coast, stopping somewhat randomly along the way. At some point, we'd heard a factory was hiring temporary workers and wiggled our way to the line of expectant day laborers. We were both picked.

Two days of standing in front of a moving belt, splitting capsicums (that's what they call bell peppers) in two. Seeds here. Flesh there. Wearing gloves and a funny cap. The heat seeping in everywhere despite the air conditioning in the giant hangar. I thought I was going to faint. The supervisor took me aside and walked me to the giant refrigerator.

"Are you okay?"

"I think so."

"You're very pale—are you pregnant?"

I wasn't. And I clearly wasn't built for this kind of work. I wasn't picked again.

We moved farther north to Cairns and spent a few weeks there, staying with a couple Craig knew from New Zealand, helping them in their car-detailing business. Amazing what you can do with toothbrushes and a water-pressure gun. It got really boring and they kept trying to bring us to their Amway meetings.

There was some magic there too. The humid heat that makes most people dart from air-conditioned car to air-conditioned pub. The mischievous possums. The giant fruit bats with doglike snouts that drop acid poop all over the cars. And we did a diving tour of the Great Barrier Reef. I got to scuba dive and pat a reef shark, put my hand in a slimy giant clam that started closing on me, and generally marvel at the rainbow of colors. I didn't want to leave the water.

We moved farther northwest, to Darwin, where we visited Litchfield national park because it was cheaper to tour than the main attraction, Kakadu, and "basically the same." Though it didn't look the same to me from the pictures. It reminded me vaguely of going out with the friend of the guy I really like . . . passing by the main dish . . .

We bought a used *Southeast Asia on a Shoestring* Lonely Planet guide and flew to Timor. Indonesia in the early nineties was the highlight of that trip. We traveled on five dollars day. That included sleep (in bamboo-partitioned homestays with occasional bedbugs), food (*nasi-goreng*, which is fried rice served on a banana leaf, though sometimes we splurged for *nasi-goreng special*, fried rice with an egg), and transport—in a packed *bemo*, the minibus of the Indonesian islands.

Indonesians are friendly and quick to smile, and they were so interested in us. Once, on a bus, my neighbor touched my arm, fascinated by the fact that I had hair there and that it was blonde. Another time, I'd declined to climb into a particularly crowded *bemo* because, truly, I could no longer stand the smoke of the clove cigarettes the men lit up constantly. When they understood why the westerner wasn't coming aboard, all the men tossed out their cigarettes and waved me in with a smile.

We island hopped for three months—the maximum amount of time allowed on the tourist visa. Craig and I kept to ourselves, following the guide book and other travelers' recommendations.

Craig never got mad, or too excited. The pace was slow, and there were many hours of not doing much—playing cards, journaling, reading paperbacks while waiting for food to be brought by a flip flop–dragging waitress.

I learned to barter, I learned to wait for hours for uber-cheap buses and trains, I learned to sit uncomfortably for hours in tiny vans, I learned to eat with my hands on a banana leaf while squatting on the side of the road, I learned to trust random people. And I learned to play backgammon.

We spent a couple weeks in Thailand, doing much of the same thing, though the vibe there was very different. I felt weary of the tourist industry after the genuine kindness and curiosity of Indonesian people.

In Bangkok, a tuk-tuk driver took us on a "scenic" ride to visit his "cousin" who would give us a special deal on gemstones, that, he guaranteed, we could sell in Europe for double the price. I sat in the little shop watching Craig go from tough-guy cynic to convinced, and convincing myself that he knew more than I did. We bought the worthless gemstones and lost about the amount Kali had given me.

And then we were off to North India.

All of this travel was amazing and eye-opening to this little Euro-centric westerner. What? People could live in a dirt-floor hut and smile? And be happy to see us, receive us? It turned my *weltanshauung* upside down. Stretched my worldview from one little country to the edges of the planet.

Sex dried out within a few weeks. As for traveling, I kept looking up to my experienced globetrotter for guidance but soon realized that his approach was not going to quench my wanderlust. Our path was definitely well beaten by hordes of Aussies and Kiwis and a sprinkling of other backpacking nationalities. I wasn't exactly sure what else I could do, but it seemed to me there could be more adventure, more ways to engage deeper with the communities we were passively cruising through.

Within a year of this bumping around, there had to be a plan of reintegrating "normal" life—meaning we both really wanted to sit on a western toilet again. Craig had no particular life plan, and because I'd committed to pick up my law studies again, we decided to move to France together.

Back in France . . .

There was no one to pick us up at the airport. No welcome home banners or special dinner or anything. I don't know what I'd expected—my dad had never been demonstrative. I couldn't even sit him down to show him the photo albums I'd made of my travels. But the worst was to find my bedroom raided. My stuff summarily packed away into the attic. The precious box I had clearly labeled "do not discard" because it contained the few treasures I possessed from my mom—rare letters, her wallet that still had some of her scent—lost.

And then to realize I had nowhere to live.

At first I had wanted to avoid Paris at all costs. Aunt Kali had a one-bedroom vacation apartment near Marseille and I'd hoped we could live there, and I could enroll to finish my law studies in the local university. But I was thwarted by some bureaucracy around registering as a returning student. I cannot remember the details, but this plan disappointingly did not pan out.

So I re-enrolled in my Paris suburban law university, and the only place we could afford to stay was at the one free place—namely, my dad's house.

The problem was, Chantal had been steadfastly working to

obtain more and more space in the house, using little Ronan as a Trojan horse, and sometimes less subtly as a ram.

When Nina turned nineteen, she moved out. She met a man ten years older than she was and left the house with a single duffle bag by climbing out the window of our grandma's granny flat. (To this day I still don't know why she didn't use the front door.) As soon as her dramatic escape was discovered, five-year-old half-brother Ronan was expelled from his room on the second floor which, apparently, Chantal urgently needed to turn into an office, and moved against his protestations into his older sister's.

Needless to say, as soon as I'd left for my disapproved-of trip, Ronan was moved into my bedroom because . . . well, I forget the justification at this point. A seven-year-old apparently needed all three upstairs bedrooms.

So Patrick offered us the attic.

Yup—I lived with my boyfriend in the attic for a year.

Now, I had loved the attic as a kid. It was filled with treasures. Suitcases full of Peruvian silver objects from my grandma's first husband. A collection of old cameras. Furniture—the old blue velour sofa bed, which became our bed, antique armoires, Chantal's table and chairs from her time as a single woman. Rows and rows of books my dad had cleverly installed on angled bookcases along the rafters, trunks with my grandma's dresses, reams of lace, boxes of my mom's Christmas decorations, old ski boots. Claire and I had smoked the last of my grandma's stale, unfiltered, gold paper–wrapped cigarettes at the Oeil-de-boeuf (oxeye window) that overlooked the backyard. Every surface, cupboard, corner was filled. And there was dust everywhere.

Somehow Craig and I were able to push a few things around. We made a space in the center for our bed and set up a kitchenette area to the side, complete with countertop stove where Craig would cook lasagna—having to just bend a little under the sloping rafters.

I finished the last year of my degree while my previously capable boyfriend floundered with language and culture.

"Good morning."

"Good morning. How did you sleep?"

"Okay . . . hey, could you help me with my homework?"

"Sure, we can look at it together this afternoon."

"No—it's due this morning . . ."

I look at the booklet. It's super basic stuff, filling out hello-how-are-you conversation bubbles. Kali generously paid for Craig to take French classes in Paris, so he'd be forced to get up in the morning, take the metro, go to the Père Lachaise neighborhood, meet people.

"But . . . you haven't done anything!" I say. "I can't be filling this out for you. It defeats the purpose! And I'll be late for class—why don't you get together with some of the other students and practice?"

"Ugh—everyone is so young there. Nobody gives a shit. The class is stupid. And it's impossible to get a job under the table here. So much fucking bureaucracy."

"Kali paid you to repaint her apartment—that was a job. Why not do that?"

"Who's gonna hire me. I don't speak French. I don't have paperwork. I don't know anyone."

I roll my eyes. "I gotta go."

I should have seen his limitations but instead I took to clamoring alongside him that it was France that was bad, the economic situation, the impossibility to get papers, to get a job, affordable housing, to, basically, live.

In contrast, according to him, New Zealand offered everything that was good and green and wholesome. And affordable.

With my undergraduate degree in sight and the heat of the approaching summer rising in the attic, the move was becoming very enticing. Everything was going to be amazing there!

So when Craig got on one knee and asked me to marry him and move to New Zealand with him, I said yes. I told myself I didn't care about marriage; I had never been a girly-girl dreaming up princess weddings. It was just a piece of paper that would allow me to live in another country (far, far away), and everything that sucked in France would be easy and perfect and amazing in New Zealand.

And I heard a voice, my own, somehow echoing inside my head: "There's always divorce!"

WITH MY EXAMS successfully passed, we got married. I easily got paperwork and we hopped back on a plane to the antipodes of France: exact opposite points of the globe. I used to joke that if I got any farther I'd actually get closer. I thought all my relationship problems were about to be solved.

Instead, soon after landing I realized that my relationship was actually over. The wholly original world traveler I'd met back on Long Island turned out to be a dime-a-dozen tall good-looking superficial nice guy from down under.

If he'd been a regular boyfriend, I'd have dumped him without much thought. But I'd just gotten married and moved terrifyingly far from home, and I was proud and pig-headed and not about to go back to my father's house, tail between my legs. So I continued to ignore the flags (I have Olympic-level abilities in that department) and set about to make it work.

And I sure grew a lot in the two years I spent navigating young-adult life in New Zealand. I earned money, paid rent. I learned to cook, started addressing back pain with yoga. Enrolled in University, acquired fluency in English.

One day, I walk into our little cottage after a day of classes. It's our second year and this is the best place we've lived in so far, with a yard and a front porch. Craig is lying inside on the couch, making it his priority, as a good native of the country, to watch endless hours of cricket.

What is cricket? Good question—though the questions that keep on bugging me are many more: How is it that I am married? How is it that I moved halfway around the world to support this man who I thought was so much older and wiser? How is it that I have three part-time jobs (teaching French, selling clothes, translating) and a full course load, and I'm encouraging him to go further with his pilot's license?

And how is it that I have zero fun with this man?

Fun was what I had with other people. University friends, especially quirky aspiring filmmaker Cosmo. And Mike's tribe.

Mike was the very first person I'd met at University of Canterbury. He wasn't a student—he was older, actually working, doing some marketing thing at the orientation fair. He struck up a conversation right away. "You're French! My wife, too, is French! Here's my number—call us up and we'll hang out! And welcome!"

Kiwis are so friendly.

Over the next two years, I hung out a fair amount with Mike, his beautiful wife, and their group of friends. They were all a bit older, more accomplished, had their shit together. I never felt like I fit quite right. But I always enjoyed Mike's company and his fun parties—and he kept on inviting me.

One memorable weekend Mike invited us to a private mountain to ski. There was no car access, so you had to walk with your gear up to the chalet that could accommodate dozens of people in rows of high bunk beds, with a huge communal kitchen and room to gather, play, goof. Skiing involved, for the babies, catching a rope with a device that looked like a nutcracker and squeezing it with both hands until you got to the top. For the serious guys (Mike and his friends), it meant hiking up the mountain with telemark skis on your back, quads of steel, and roaming freely.

Back home with Craig, I had tried and tried and nothing had worked. The handsome young guy I had met in the US now had hunched shoulders, atrophied muscles from inactivity, and stale traveling stories I had heard a hundred times.

"Let's go skiing this weekend!" I'd say.

"I hate skiing."

"Let's go camping!"

"We don't have any gear."

"Let's go out to dinner tonight."

"It's not in the budget."

"Well, we need to do something together. That's what couples do. We need to share new experiences together. What would you like to do?"

" . . . "

I bought a copy of *Men Are from Mars, Women Are from Venus*. Got really hopeful—"oh! I'm just not communicating effectively with this alien! It's just a new language to learn!" I'd follow him around the house reading him quotes. I started saying, "Would you please take the garbage out" instead of "could you" because, of course, men can physically take the garbage out. It's just that they want to know they are doing it of their own volition.

I begged Craig to read the book. He didn't. I'd place it stealthily on different surfaces in the apartment, obvious but not too obvious, but he never opened it. It felt to me like a deliberate refusal to grow with me. I couldn't understand it.

After almost two and a half years of dogged head-down efforting with my relationship, I suddenly didn't care anymore. Come what may. I felt something—or someone—stir inside of me, something not-me that felt steely and powerful. Perhaps I'd been invaded by a dark monstress, and she scared me. I couldn't look at her—but I didn't have the energy to hold her back.

And then there was one of those days you can only have in your twenties, I think, a particular energy vortex of freedom and carefreeness. Mike's birthday prompting a few friends to blow off responsibilities for the day. To go ice skating, which is very conducive to holding hands and grabbing hips. To gather at someone's house, to sit on the front porch together while the others stay inside.

To kiss.

Did I mention Mike was hot? Blue eyes, curly blond hair, quick to laugh. He was witty and funny and always up to some exciting adventure. He also had a tiny stutter when he got nervous that made him seem tender in contrast to his tall, hard body. It made me want to kiss him like crazy.

I had an affair. At twenty-three, the very word cracked me up. It seemed so ridiculous. First of all to be married, but then to have an affair! Seemed so grown up and old-fashioned and completely alien. I barely felt married. I barely felt that I was in a relationship. There was nothing going on there.

But oh, on the other side . . . there was a man who saw me. "The world is your oyster" he'd said to me at a pre-affair lunch once. I hadn't fully understood the expression so he'd explained it with other things I couldn't really grasp either, like, "You can do anything you want" (I can?) and "New Zealand is too small for you" (for little me?). He also wanted me, his physical desire unequivocally expressed with his eyes, hands, breath.

Yet he made it clear nothing "serious" would happen between us. Sitting at the little table in the backyard of his hillside house, surrounded by dark green foliage, he explained to me his theory of marriage. He put his hands in a circle and said: "Marriage is like a pie." He drew a triangle shape and said, "You can't get all the pieces of the pie from one person." Then he curled his fingers as if he was retrieving a slice of said pie. "For instance, the sex piece is missing. So you go get it elsewhere."

I was the piece of ass in his pie.

I nodded understanding, only causing more fogginess in my clouded, infatuated brain, and I proceeded to stop eating and sleeping.

I began to function only insofar as it involved Mike. I seemed to be operating from a program I didn't know was installed in me.

I'd known him as a friend for two and a half years—and it all came down to two crazy weeks.

Getting sexually involved with Mike gave me access to some internal fuel I didn't know I possessed. I did things I had no idea I was capable of. I biked for an hour to get to his place—and back again—though my back often plagued me with sharp pains.

I went in the freezing Pacific ocean to swim alongside him, even though it would take my body two hours to warm up again.

I lied about my whereabouts.

To my husband. To his wife.

The compulsion to be with him was so overpowering, it simply had to be love.

I completely disassociated from myself. I shut my ears to the little voice that was trying to point out how similar this felt to what my stepmother had done. I was technically a friend to Mike's wife. How could I look her in the eyes?

There was a party the weekend after Mike and I had started seeing each other. I don't know why I went. Perhaps it would have looked suspicious for me to flake. Perhaps it was the thrill of being near him, no matter the circumstance.

I am sitting on the big white couch in his living room, in her living room. The usual bunch of friends is gathered and Mike is nearby, within reach. I experience the chemistry between us as a huge, palpable beast. I am scared of moving, or catching his eye. The pressure is so intense I split. I leave my body and suddenly I am seeing the whole scene from above: hands gesturing, heads laughing. I am floating outside of me.

I don't know how I got through work, homework, everything was a blur other than the moments with him. And there were precious few moments. Just a few days of pure, white-hot excitement.

I can't help running up the dirt path that leads from the road to his house, hidden in lush vegetation. I know the way to the back door—he showed me. When I walk in, he is doing push-ups. His t-shirt is drenched with sweat.

"You're early!" He smiles—a little embarrassed. But he jumps up and holds me. My nose in his chest inhales his sweat and I swoon. Unfortunately, he pulls away to go change his shirt. I stand in the middle of the living room, having no clue what to do. But he comes right back and grabs me. We kiss, gently at first, then picking up the pace, hands everywhere, breathing heavy. We fall to the floor. He lifts me onto the nearby beanbag. Clothing is peeled off—bottoms only. I can't even process what is happening. He is in me, then he comes. He laughs. "Sorry—I was way too much in a rush. Come, let's do it properly." He picks me up and takes me to the guest room. There is a huge window with a view of the Sumner Bay. A ray of sun warms the bed. This time we undress fully—and he makes love to my whole body.

Between work, and weekends where we couldn't be alone,

this happened only a few more times. And then poof, he was gone on the six-week skiing trip to North America he'd been planning with his best friends for ages.

Mike had said repeatedly nothing more would happen between us. But then he emailed me. And again. I started living for his emails. Turning on the iMac at my university office, feverishly waiting for the hourglass icon on the screen to disappear, for the web browser to open, for Yahoo email to load up. He wrote every time: "Make sure to delete this message!"

And I did.

But for one.

There was one . . . a long email describing his awe-filled experience in Whistler, listening to Leftfield Leftism (I ran straight to the university store, bought the album and played it on a loop) and the thoughts he was having of me. I printed the email. I needed to read it again and again.

And maybe I needed it to be found.

One night, I went out with Cosmo and other university friends. When I came back, Craig had rummaged through my backpack and found the email. Everything after that was quite ridiculous. He broke my Leftfield CD, locked me out of the house, called Mike's wife. I got on my bike and, on my way to Cosmo's house, looked up. The night was clear, a trillion southern-hemisphere stars scintillating in the blue-black of the sky. My lips broke into a huge smile. Mike's words came back: "New Zealand is too small for you—the world is your oyster." I felt I belonged to the universe.

I packed my backpack with the few things that mattered—the photo of my mom, the printed emails—and left everything else I'd built there without looking back. I acquiesced like you bat away a fly to the financial demands of my disgruntled soon-to-be-ex who, though I had clamored about the upcoming demise of our relationship for, well, two and a half years, could take no responsibility for the situation. He was a simple guy comforted by the simple fact that I was, after all, French, and therefore sexually loose. What else could he have expected?

I walked away.

Actually I flew—New Zealand is an island. Staying was not an option considering the wave of ill feelings coming at me from our community. I bought a ticket back to France, with a week layover in San Francisco because, damn it, the world was my oyster and that's where I'd wanted to go in the first place. I vaguely figured I'd get a job back in Paris . . . and mostly, bolstered by the belief that I thought I was in actual love this time, I clung to the possibility of seeing my lover again.

CHAPTER FIVE

Morass

Aunt Kali had a one-bedroom apartment near the Canal St. Martin in the 10th arrondissement. In my late teens, I had loved that place as a sweet retreat from my dad's house. Big windows overlooking a landscaped courtyard, white walls, plush deep blue carpet throughout, always barefoot, always warm. Kali understood why I'd prefer to stay with her rather than at her brother's house in the suburbs, and she welcomed me in even though we had to share her bed. For a couple months it was fun. We'd sink side by side into the velvety chocolate-brown sofa to study the movie times and write out weekly activities in our "synoptic calendar" as she called it.

She circled job ads for me in the paper and I made a few phone calls, but she'd worked as a social security doctor for the last thirty years and neither of us had any job-hunting or networking skills. I tried to see Claire but felt disconnected from her tribe of Beaux-Arts graduates. I couldn't seem to reintegrate into French life. I had no moorings there. I was too mad at my mom's family for abandoning me after her death. And I was too mad at my dad for . . . being my dad, I guess.

And every morning, I woke up thinking of Mike and marveling at my capacity to love so much at such distance and for so long (months!) and in the clear knowledge that nothing, nothing was ever going to happen (though secret fantasies ran on a loop in my mind).

Kali was trying her best to support me. She made me write out a checklist of qualities one should look for in a man. The mistake we had made with Craig (she always said "we"—she, too, had loved his sweetness and had been greatly disappointed) was that he wasn't educated. So top of the list would be an educated man. He would have to be not just smart but an intellectual. A highly accomplished intellectual herself, my aunt was a cliché of snobbishness. It was good comedy at times. Good manners, good family . . . I think we hit all the conventional line items. Oh, and he would have to be in love with me more than I was with him.

Mike definitely did not fit that last one.

Kali and I had some good times, and I tried to tell myself that this was a new chapter, that I had come back from my antipodian adventure wiser and more equipped for the world—highly marketable, in fact! I was going to find a great job and begin my adult life. But my enthusiasm was fading. The reality of job hunting and the almost complete absence of social network, then Kali giving up her apartment and retiring to her little studio in the south left me no choice but to . . . move back in with my dad.

Again.

This time, my grandma having died, I got placed in the granny flat, street level with its own private door, and it somehow felt even creepier than the attic.

Here I am, working at the reception of the clinic. I know every step from the house to this place. I know exactly what to do—processing incoming and outgoing patients, paging doctors.

"Ding-ding," I press the clinic-wide intercom button, turn on the mellifluous voice: "Monsieur So-and-So, you are expected in the lobby. Monsieur So-and-So, please make your way to the lobby." And I'm thinking, "Am I twenty-three? or am I sixteen?

Did I have a dream about moving to another country?" Everything is so familiar, yet out of focus. The thought of myself as an independent, money-earning, rent-paying, married adult seems distant, unlikely. Maybe I never left. This is my summer job. I am sixteen. I live under my father's roof with my evil stepmother yelling daily at her son whom I adore as my little brother.

And I want to die.

Nothing has changed.

That pull to die, I had successfully buried during my time in New Zealand. Fresh air, space, and nature's raw beauty had helped. I had felt things there—experienced sensations, in my body, my own emerging Self. I had created a life and I had wanted to live! But back in the suburban town, steeped in what Claire still calls "the micro-climate of doom," I just wanted to disappear. I'd get up just in time to go to work. Cross the street, settle behind the reception desk. Work, come home. What did I do in the evenings? On weekends? I don't remember talking to anyone other than my dad and stepmother. I tried to pretend that I was an equal, but I felt like a little girl.

I didn't know why—I just could not function there. I couldn't come up with a plan to leave, to do anything else, ever. I had even (almost) successfully shut down the lover fantasies.

The one scenario that kept coming up, providing some solace, was death. Drowning, I was convinced, would be the best way to go—I'd always been a water creature. It seemed it would be warm and painless, a gentle return to the womb. There was the pool at the clinic, where I'd learned to swim as a baby, or the municipal pool. But the logistics were challenging. Enter after closing hours? Use weights? I entertained pills, which seemed more expedient, but Kali had failed twice in the ten years since her son committed suicide, and she was a doctor so that put a dent in my confidence.

Then I got a phone call.

From New Zealand.

This is 1998 in France. No social network, lucky if I had occasional Internet access. For him to find me, my dad's land line number, and to actually call me internationally, seemed plain extraordinary.

"Evelyne . . . it's Mike."

" . . . "

"Evelyne? Can you hear me?"

"Mike . . . hi . . ."

We catch up on our whereabouts. Our current life situation. And then:

"I'm living on my own. We tried to make it work for months. She was devastated—she suffered so much from my betrayal. She's going back to live in France. We're getting a divorce."

My heart is pounding. I cannot look at the pain I have caused Mike's hapless wife. A friend. She had been a friend to me. I cannot stop to look at that. I hear only what I narrowly focus on hearing.

He is single!

Mike continues:

"You have no idea how much shit I took from our friends. Everyone was on my case for making such a mess. I won't tell you what they said about you being a homewrecker . . ."

I apply myself to ignoring that.

There is hope! He is getting a divorce! And he is calling me. Me!

"I'd love to see you if that's ever possible again," he says. My heart jumps for joy. "The thought of your body . . . what we could do . . ." At that, I get a little deflated. But I ignore it.

Then he asks about me. I don't want to fess up that I am in a pitiful state, but he knows me enough to perceive the despair underneath my mumbled answers.

"Evelyne. You don't belong there. You have to leave. Do you have money?"

Just two days before, I'd opened an official-looking letter from the lawyer who had been handling my grandmother's estate since her death two years prior. There was a check in it—with my name on it.

"Yes."

"You get out of there. Now. You pack your bags, you buy a plane ticket. You leave. Promise me you will."

The money wasn't huge but it was enough to tell my dad I was leaving. He disapproved, of course, as he'd always disapproved of anything that was my own will that he couldn't control.

Once again, he couldn't stop me and he knew it, and it made him (and his wife) furious. There was yelling. They accused me of being the cause of their son's repeated need for therapy (what? huh?) and told me, as usual, that my departure denoted my instability and incapacity to make mature decisions.

I was just fleeing for my life.

And toward, I thought, true love.

CHAPTER SIX
Husband #2

With my grandma's money, I bought a ticket to Australia. My official reasoning was such: I want to go back to "that region in the world where I have been happy." I couldn't go back to Christchurch because I was persona non grata there. And it would be a little too obvious what I was doing there. It didn't occur to me there were other towns I could have gone to in that country. I told myself that Australia was close enough. I'd vaguely heard someone say that with New Zealand residency, you could work in Australia. That was good enough a plan for me.

I had:

- no contacts
- no job prospects
- no idea of the paperwork actually required
- no place to sleep upon landing, or thereafter

In October of 1998, I am twenty-three, divorced, with fifteen thousand francs to my name, on a plane to Australia. That's my life.

In flight, I befriended the French girl sitting next to me. Stephanie was bravely off to backpack Australia by herself and was thrilled to meet such an experienced traveler as myself. She was also much more organized than I was and had actually booked a hostel in Sydney. We paired up naturally.

She begged me to travel with her for a bit. Since I had some money and was not in a super hurry to get a job, I bought a Greyhound ticket and hopped on her bus.

All it would take would be a phone call, an email, a snap of his fingers, and I'd be right back next to Mike. Or on top. Or underneath.

Or perhaps he would come get me instead. He was a seasoned traveler; it would be nothing to him. That was the true, though unavowed, "plan."

Off I went on the Greyhound. I loved Australia's outbacks. The vastness and the palpable ancientness of the landscape. Traveling with Craig a few years before, we'd made the decision to stick to the East Coast. I felt I had missed out on the vast Red Center, and Uluru, the 550-million-year-old sandstone formation sacred to the Aboriginals. I felt empowered, coming back by myself to complete this.

On the way, however, just a few days into the trip, Steph and I made an overnight stop in the backpackers' hostel of a little mining town named Broken Hill. As the bus was driving through the main street, I noticed a cute guy with a guitar taking money out at the ATM. Sure enough, as we checked into the hostel, there he was.

He engaged with us right away in the communal kitchen. Steph was quickly lost—her English wasn't good enough for Scott's American humor and sharp wit. He was kind of short, and younger than me by a couple years, which made me almost instantly dismiss him. But there was an attractive intensity about him. I also liked—spoiler alert!—the cropped blond hair and gentle blue eyes behind the little rectangles of his glasses, and the permanent American grin complete with defined jawline and perfect white teeth.

He was on a world-round trip, a gift from his dad on graduating (early) from Harvard. He seemed delighted to hang out with me. He spoke a mile a minute and kept making jokes and flashing his pearly whites. I could barely keep up.

I also remember him saying, "I want to make a ton of money one day!" and letting out high-pitched, self-amused laughter. I'd never heard anyone say that. Let alone say it so casually, like it was a possibility. Yeah, I thought. His energy was contagious.

"Are you going to see the meteors tonight?"

Of course I knew nothing about meteors. This guy actually informed himself outside of the Lonely Planet guide.

"Come with me—I found the best place in town to watch them. It's one in a hundred years!"

It was clear Steph was not invited.

I can still remember the thoughts going through my mind. I was on this trip partly in defiance of Craig who couldn't make it happen, so I was proving to myself that I could travel alone (ish) and go where the hell I wanted to. I was here also because I had hoped for Mike to come get me, but since there had been no indication of him coming, I'd wanted to prove my independence (ish) rather than sit around in Sydney waiting for him.

And now I was checking boxes on the list Kali and I had established. Unlike husband #1, this guy was well educated—even I had heard of Harvard. He was obviously smart and definitely an intellectual. I mean: he was Jewish! He also clearly moved around the world with the ease of someone coming from money. I called Kali to report on my trip (and run this guy by her) and even she was impressed. He was definitely a winner at the box-checking game.

As night fell, we clambered up the one little knoll of Broken Hill and watched the meteors. I'd never seen such enormous fireballs, some with obvious tails, criss-crossing the night sky of the southern hemisphere. And Scott was so entertaining—firing up a storm of questions about me, about what I liked, about the universe. His energy was so different from Craig's (who had next to none.) He was, flatteringly, obviously into me. He seemed smitten by the aura of the "older French divorcee."

There were great moments of high and excitement and hope—yet I don't think my heart was ever fully in it. It makes me so sad to think back on that. But I believed I had followed my heart before and it had gotten me nowhere. Well, it had gotten me away from my dad and having already lived a lifetime by twenty-three, but what a mess I'd made.

We spent the night together in his bottom bunk, making out heavily although he refused to go all the way, which completely baffled me. I wasn't aware yet of the complicated American hangups around sex. But he did say with an unshakable certainty that rattled me, "I want you in my life."

I was intrigued and attracted and tickled pink by his attention, but I was also determined to get on my way and travel alone —without a man, that is. The next morning, though he begged me to stay, I got back on the bus with Steph. He walked me to the stop, and as I was climbing the Greyhound steps, he handed me a ripped page from his journal with all the ways in which I could reach him. I think it even had his dad's phone number.

I forget now the details of that journey. I remember having a radar for Internet cafes where I'd feverishly check my inbox. It was nerve-wracking because you had to pay by the minute and I was such a slow typer. I would first scan for an email from Mike. Most of the time, nothing. But there would usually be something from Scott and it felt . . . nice. He was a good writer, sharing experiences and feelings with sensibility and depth. On a few occasions there was a message from Mike. Hope battered the inside of my rib cage then. But every time, it was disappointing— something about wanting to fuck me, or imagining me on this fabulous trip freely fucking. Nothing about coming to meet me.

One day, there was a particularly beautiful email from Scott. It was his guided tour of the town Stephanie and I were passing through, and it involved a treasure hunt. Stay in this hostel, visit these gardens, have an ice cream in that place (and here's why). Then go to the record store next door, find the U2 album on aisle three, look up the last song.

Steph and I followed the directions. She loved my whole story of New-York-travel-marriage-New Zealand-lover. She'd closely followed the Scott "thing" and was an agreeable sounding board for the Mike vs. Scott debate. The scales were tipping fast and she became a joyful cheerleader on our little town tour. We had ice cream. Then got to the record store, aisle three, and found the album. We quickly scanned for the title of the last song, and both gushed when we read: "All I Want Is You."

I went a little farther on the trip with her but eventually said au revoir and headed for Melbourne, where Scott had most recently been staying. I felt pulled by a rope tethered to the center of me, to my very insides. It was a choiceless act. I felt compelled, directed. I thought it was romantic love. I was, once more, enamored by the story.

A thorn in that story was the name of the backpacker's hostel where he was staying: "Toad Hall." Really? That wasn't befitting of my romance. Unless, of course, that is where princesses go to kiss their prince. I found the place easily. I hadn't announced my arrival by email, for whatever reason, and had no way of knowing if Scott was still staying there. I pinned a message on the crowded cork board.

He got it.

For days after our reunion he would, at random times, while walking down the street for instance, jump into the air and yell, "I can't believe you're here!" or "I'm so happy you're here!"

It was infectious.

At night as we cuddled in a shared bunk, he'd say, "Thank you."

"For what?"

"Thank you for spending this day with me."

I was constantly surprised by him.

To hell with my plans of finding a job in Australia . . . I now set my sights on America.

◈

I traveled with Scott until I was close to running out of money.

Hong Kong, January 1st, 1999. Scott has a brilliant idea:

"Let's go to China. Beijing."

"I don't know . . . I'm not really feeling it."

"But when's the next time we'll be so close to China, huh? What's the likelihood of us getting back to this corner of the world anytime soon?"

"Good point."

"There's a train. It's cheap. We can sleep in it."

We got on the train.

A thirty-hour ride in a dirty compartment with no access to food (there was no restaurant). Besides, westerners were not allowed to leave their assigned wagon. We had brought a box of cereal to munch on and made do. The toilet was a hole you had to squat over while watching the tracks zoom by beneath your butt, and that you had to ask the attendant permission to use. Good thing there was nothing to eat.

I was already used to following Scott blindly. He was the planner, the reader, the strategist. It was so refreshing to be with someone who'd gather multiple data points on a place and determine the most original way to experience it.

We arrived at the Beijing main station late at night. We had no yuan. And no way to get any. Scott had assumed that any major transport hub would have the modern conveniences we'd come to expect as world travelers, such as ATMs. Not so in Beijing. For starters, no westerners took the train from Hong Kong. Normal people flew into the city.

We were swarmed by hawkers. That was not an unusual experience for backpackers, but these people were obviously unaccustomed to westerners, and spoke no English. Somehow, with a combination of gestures and yelling "hotel! hotel!" we took a leap of faith and climbed into a driver's van. The drive went on. And on. We were looking at each other, telepathically convincing each other that we were going to be robbed and left naked on the side of the road.

Did I mention it was January?

January. In Beijing.

Traveling with a handful of monsoon-season clothes for tropical Asia.

I tore my blue sarong in half so each of us could have a makeshift scarf to prevent some of the icy air from freezing our lips and noses.

Eventually, the van arrived at a decent-looking hotel. The receptionist spoke some English. We were able to change money at a ridiculous rate. And we had to hand over our passports in order to spend the night.

Scott called his daddy the next day and we transferred to the Holiday Inn near the airport. It was a large complex of shops and restaurants, clearly made for westerners who needed to avoid as much of Beijing as possible.

For the next ten days, we took the ten a.m. shuttle to the McDonald's on Tiananmen square, then walked nonstop for five or six hours. We returned on the same shuttle exhausted, skin cracking from the dry cold, and starving, debating if we should have Swiss, Indian, or "Continental" for dinner.

We found it impossible to communicate with anyone. Taxi drivers seemed incapable of reading a map, so pointing at a destination was a lost cause. We managed to buy a couple of hats on the street but couldn't figure out street food. On my 24th birthday, I was skating on the frozen lake of the Summer palace. On the day we made it to the Great Wall, all I remember is my torn sarong freezing solid in front of my mouth. Then the ATM ate my card, the bank attendants inside gesticulated until I gave up trying to understand, and I became wholly dependent on Scott.

We flew to Bangkok the next day.

I had no particular love for that town that I found crawling with westerners interested in the lowliest of the sex trade, and locals interested in any ways they could extract money from westerners.

It was hot and humid. Our room had one fan and no window. We had taken refuge in the downstairs Internet cafe. Scott was only a few months into the trip he'd planned for the year.

"Let's go to India!"

I broke into tears. "You go. I'm going back to France. Look me up when you're done."

I was bluffing, of course—what the hell was I going to do in France? Perhaps Aunt Bathilde, in Paris, would come through for me, but I wasn't very confident I could ask her anything. I just couldn't go on pretending I was a moneyed globetrotter leisurely whiling away the months.

It worked. He wanted me more than he wanted the traveling. He called up his dad and said he was flying back home with someone special.

And a whole new kind of wonderful and scary started for me.

We flew to France for a bit. I wanted Aunt Kali to meet

Scott, to get her stamp of approval. I also wanted to parade him to my dad, show him I was going to be okay.

It was a terrible mistake.

I called him from a phone booth.

"Hi, Patrick! It's me, your daughter."

"Oh, you're here, are you?"

"Yes! We're in Paris. I want to come visit so you can meet Scott."

"Who?"

"Scott, you know, I told you. Last time we spoke? The American guy I met traveling? The Harvard guy."

"I don't know who that is. Anyway, you know when I'm home."

My heart is sinking but I forge ahead with hope:

"Okay, then we'll come by tomorrow afternoon, okay?"

"Whatever you wanna do."

The next day Scott and I make our way via the same metro line I used to take as a teenager to escape into the city. The house is dark. Metal shutters on all the windows sealed closed. I ring the bell. My dad opens the door. "Oh, you came."

"Yeah . . . I mean, I said I would . . ."

We step into the dark house. And then the details escape me, though the unpleasant sensation from that encounter has imprinted itself on me. Maybe there is an unfriendly offer of drinks. Something in me explodes. Heated words fire out of my mouth. I storm up the stairs to fill a bag with random things I feel belong rightfully to me. I intend never to set foot in the house again. Patrick follows me with his own insane recriminations about my abandoning him, them, I don't know. Scott follows silently, eyes wide. We are back downstairs with a duffle full of books, a picture or two, some clothes, an old lovey. And my uncle's antique banjo. I walk through the front door, right past my dad. Scott pauses, and Patrick politely shakes his hand and wishes him bon voyage.

✥

Nineteen ninety-nine saw me flying between the US and France and passing through the US border a number of times. Legit humans with navy blue passports get their stamps and walk right on to baggage claim. Shady characters like me, mid-twenties, traveling alone on repeat tourist visas, get sent to secondary screening along with my luggage, which was thoroughly searched.

I didn't even try to pretend that it was normal for tourists to carry framed photos of their moms and folders full of emails (I'd printed our conversations and organized them in plastic sleeves). The border officer read a few and was obviously enjoying himself. "Wow," he said, "that guy's a good writer."

I played the romantic card. Yes, he is my boyfriend and yes, I am in love with him, but NO! I have no intention of marrying him and moving to the US. My life is in France, my whole family is in France! Then he found the plate of negatives that Claire had taken of me. She'd used me as a model for practicing drawing when she was at the Ecole des Beaux-Arts, and again for her photography. One exhibit was called "Pin-ups": she'd had the idea of juxtaposing taxidermied animals to a naked female body. Also a fresh pig's head straight from the butcher. Upon my asking, she had also taken dozens of photographs of me sexy-posing on her couch with an open bathrobe, or nothing. I had originally thought to send the photos to Mike, but that was before Australia. I wasn't sure if it was right to give them to Scott when he hadn't been the intended recipient. I didn't even think I looked that good. The officer took the plates and disappeared, leaving me to count my heartbeats per second. He came back after about fifteen minutes.

"Okay, miss, you can be on your way."

He helped me repack my bag as I tripped over myself with thank yous.

I finally arrived at John Wayne airport in Orange County and was greeted by bursts of joy from Scott . . . and a beautiful blonde woman who embraced me and handed me a furry bear. Scott's stepmom Melba became my champion and first best friend in America.

We piled into the Range Rover and headed for the nine-thousand-square-foot house on a hill overlooking the Pacific Ocean in Laguna Beach.

I had landed in a Hollywood movie.

We spent a few months at Roy and Melba's house, pretending to look for jobs. We'd leave the house (and poolside) only to go to the grocery store. We'd concoct elaborate dinners during which Roy and Scott would butt heads on the subject of jobs.

"How's the job search?"

"Well, I don't know Dad, I might want to be a writer."

"You're just pissed that I published a book before you."

"That was a business book, Dad. I want to write a real book."

"Are you writing? I don't see you writing. Writers write."

Next day:

"How's the job search?"

"I want to be a woodworker. I want to do stuff like Sam Maloof."

The next day:

"So Scooter, I called up Sam Maloof. Really nice guy. We talked for half an hour. He's willing to meet you and consider an internship."

Everything, with Roy, was an actual possibility.

I couldn't understand why nothing was coalescing for Scott. Instead, he was finding more and more reasons why California sucked. At the dinner table in the giant open-floor living room framed by the landscaped pool (with waterfall) on one side and the ocean on the other, Scott and his dad argued with increasing tension about the pros and cons of California. Melba always tried to moderate. I tried to be loyal to Scott's point of view.

Eventually Scott's Chicago uncle got him a job in a tech company in which he sat on the board. We got a U-Haul and drove across the country to a loft in a converted shoe factory near the river. A giant red-brick building with floor-to-ceiling windows and sturdy original wooden beams. I felt übercool.

I applied for a student visa and funneled the last of my money into a sad downtown "university" that admitted me in the 2000 spring semester and allowed me to stay legally for a year. The visa permitted me to work only on campus, which meant I could be exploited. I taught English to Chinese MBA students in the language center for seven dollars an hour, which meant I was almost entirely dependent on my Harvard man and his fancy tech job (and the checks from his family).

At the end of my student year, we were faced with the visa question again. The options were to live in France (it was out of the question for him) or to separate (neither of us wanted that) or to . . .

"Let's get married," I believe is the way it went. It wasn't a romantic proposal but at least it came from him. And this time I didn't tell myself, "There's always divorce!"

At least not immediately.

I loved his intellect, his wit. We'd spend hours cuddling on the couch, diving deep into trying to figure out life, ourselves, our dreams. Making random plans for the future such as, we'd move to Montana and live on a ranch, or to Los Angeles and he'd become a famous actor. France had made me feel stifled with its rigid expectations about what is "done" or simply isn't done. With Scott, I was intoxicated by the ever-present hint of the possible.

We were really good friends and had a lot of fun together. He was curious and excited about a lot of things, as was I, and it was wonderful to have a companion who'd get off the couch and plan things. And had money.

I also adored his family. I had loved my previous mother-in-law and it was partly her sweetness that had kept me longer in the marriage. But this was a whole other level. I wanted so badly to be part of that family (of any family, you could point out, and it wouldn't be untrue).

I discovered the world of Chicago bar mitzvahs. We hung out a lot at the stately, professionally decorated brownstone of Scott's Aunt Shelley and Uncle Mark. Or we'd meet them for brunch at the Four Seasons.

Roy and his sister Shelley talked on the phone regularly. Everyone in that family talked on the phone regularly. They seemed so together and not all broken up and dysfunctional like my whacko family. They read how-to books. They sought out help for their kid who was struggling in school. They were devoted to their kids' well-being. It was a huge learning curve for me to live amongst people who communicated deeply and cared about self-improvement.

We had a simple marriage ceremony in the backyard of the brownstone. I was twenty-six, got a social security number, and began to feel like a human member of society. And, without ever fessing up to Roy that he'd been right, we drove back to California.

Chapter Seven
Pain and Pleasure in LaLa Land

The layout of Los Angeles is so befuddling to a European. The sheer size requiring hours in the car, the absence of workable mass transit, the inhumane width of streets and the weird dead zones between neighborhoods . . . I couldn't wrap my head around it. But Scott took it on with his usual enthusiasm. He bought a guidebook on his favorite topic, food, and with *CounterIntelligence* in hand we explored the city and I began to love . . . parts of it.

We found a one-bedroom near Sunset and LaBrea that had a rooftop pool, and I let the sun wash over me and feed the depressed cells of my brain. I was just beginning to trust that, maybe, this was it—I could settle. Build something.

Scott was optimistic about all the things he was going to accomplish here. I got a marketing job in an organic grocery store and, with the various checks from his mom, dad, and grandmother, he could take some time to figure out what he wanted to do.

I sometimes wondered if the checks were more a curse than a blessing. I had never lacked money growing up—it simply wasn't something we talked about. But we also didn't have the kind of consumerist behavior that I was watching unfold in Scott.

First, there was music. He'd spend hours reading about musicians and new albums, and buying CDs. At first I'd been enthusiastic about this passion. But then I got frustrated—how did he have the time for this?

There were books too. Books I could never argue with. In fact, I never argued about anything—there was no convincing Scott that we didn't need the latest thing he desired. I could delay it, but only for a bit. There was always something "we" needed.

The camera (which is forbidden to be used for silly family videos, meaning it never got used). Speakers. Computer. Electronics. Software. Organizers for all the things we bought. (They have stores dedicated to organizing in America!) Tools to set up shelves for the stuff we bought. Shelves.

But mostly I didn't really know where the money was going. Because we didn't have to worry about it, I didn't pay attention. I trusted him. My first salary was thirty thousand dollars a year. We got about as much from his family. I was puzzled that we didn't seem able to save—I would have liked to start a fund to buy a house. But Scott kept resisting and the money kept flowing out.

Intimacy-wise, we were comfortable with each other's bodies. I learned the term "cuddle buddy"—and we were great ones, bingeing on *Band of Brothers* on the couch. We took showers together. We worked out together. We experimented with various diets. Scott had been a pudgy kid and was always struggling to rein in weight gain. I always felt I had five too many pounds.

But sex . . . at least the sex that I kept dreaming was possible or even "should" happen between people in their mid-twenties, that was elusive. I had images of the puppies that were born in the house I grew up in, playing and piling up to sleep close to each other. But I didn't feel like a desired woman.

One day on the phone with Claire, I tentatively opened a conversation around intimacy.

"Sex is the glue!" she said. "I need it to function. If we don't do it, I don't feel bonded to him, and I get grumpy. He knows it well. Every four or five days I start to lose it and he jokes, 'ah! she needs her [rude French expression involving dick and injection]!'"

Four to five days.

I'm scanning for the last time we did it. A month? No I'm pretty sure it was about six weeks. Certainly not memorable. In fact—none of our sexual encounters are, come to think of it. We do it as an afterthought, sometimes because I complain. Is there orgasm? I'm not even sure. There is a localized event, an energetic release, but nothing that overcomes me or shuts down my mind.

In fact, in order to come, I have to go completely into my mind. I have to disappear from this body, his body, and make up stories.

But the scripts are disturbing and I don't want to think about it anymore than just for the brief instant it helps me finish the act. They're also limited and involve various forms of defilement. I'd read a memoir that had caused a ruckus in France, titled *The Sexual Life of Catherine M.* In it the author described her encounters with faceless and countless dicks at night in a public park. I replayed that scenario.

Another one was to be taken in a public place, by a random man I might have been vaguely attracted to in a restaurant. It would be a stealth, though public, act. He is barely paying attention to me while laboring over my behind, and I pretend that nothing is going on as I am bent over the table. No one else is taking notice. It's quick and then it's over.

But possibly even more disturbing, and therefore unacknowledged, was the script with another man in bed. I'm on my back. Scott is on top of me.

And behind him is the other man.

Taking him.

I am revolted by the thought, and revolted by the fact that the thought gets me off. I put all my energies into drawing the iron curtain back down, get the whole thing over with, and go back to Damian Lewis for the next few weeks.

Sometimes I get off in the shower. The first thing I do when moving into an American place is go buy a handheld shower with pressure controls. I put the jet straight on my clitoris and imagine a disembodied cock penetrating me. It is neither pleasurable nor sensuous but it makes me come and I feel some relief. I do that quickly and silently in the fear of being caught and then avoid thinking about it.

It came to a point where I felt that I repulsed him. I already had a lot of hate for my body and acted on it in a lot of weird, very subtle ways. Using strange rules and calculations to limit my food intake, use of electric power, toilet paper consumption. Exercising in painful ways in order to force change upon this evidently flawed body.

It pains me so much to write this. If you'd seen me in my twenties it wouldn't have occurred to you that there was anything to complain about. I beg my body daily now for forgiveness for the mistreatment and violence I heaved upon it all these years.

But perhaps I, too, was a bit repulsed by him. His constant struggle with food and exercise. The way he'd put both hands on his scalp and scratch rapidly, head bent forward so the dandruff would fall on the table. The subtle way in which he conveyed disapproval of my behind's curve if I hadn't worked out enough. Or when I tried wearing things other than athletic cotton underwear. The way he'd touch my body as if it was a teddy bear.

I was mad at him too for his inability to focus and commit

to a career. By then I'd started working at an elite environmental organization I had been a member of since Chicago. I'd quit the marketing "director" job at the grocery store to take an internship with NRDC—the office director had been surprised at what she saw as a step down for me, but she didn't realize I would have done anything to start working for a cause I believed in.

My first job was to collect data on diesel exhaust from school buses. Turns out, idling buses at schools mornings and afternoons might be bad for kids' lungs. Policy changes require the craziest science. I'd get up at three or four in the morning and drive to the edge of L.A. and surrounding counties to arrive at the "randomly selected school" in order to record how long buses left their engines on. Then I'd find a public park or McDonald's to wait around with my LSAT practice book, and do the same thing as school let out.

After a couple months, NRDC cut me a check for $1,600 dollars. I'd never earned so much money! I was so proud—and they offered me a job as a paralegal. I had finally landed a real life.

But Scott . . . Scott wasn't progressing. He suddenly decided he was going to be a filmmaker, go to film school, and absolutely needed a Sony digital camera to make short films.

The camera cost $1,600.

The sex topic stayed on the back burner. Besides, my back, who'd been yelling at me daily for close to ten years, was now screaming for attention. I began a desperate quest for relief.

I appeared flexible and athletic, the yoga-type in touch with her mind–body. But inside I was in constant conversation with my old friend: pain. She never left me. The energy it took to deny her and prove that I could do stuff in spite of her was exhausting. And yet if I didn't feel her for a moment, I would tweak my back a little to the side and pow! Yep, there she was, a sharp burst in the lower part of my spine, radiating exquisitely up the back and down the legs.

I would go to yoga classes and do all sorts of cool bendy things. Then I couldn't get up from the mat. One day we were sitting cross-legged for meditation and I noticed my hands could not reach my knees. I didn't realize that my back muscles were so seized up they prevented me from even bending my head forward. I just assumed my arms were too short.

I would bike to work, sit in an office chair all day, bike back and collapse flat on the bedroom floor, oftentimes passing out for half an hour before being able to have a life in the evening.

I tried jogging with Scott because he insisted cardio was the only way to stay thin, but walking was excruciating for days after. Same when I went dancing—but I loved dancing so much I accepted the trade-off.

I had told myself for so long that everyone had pain—that's what it was to be alive in a body. But it was becoming clear that my friends did not deal with that. And that white-knuckling through the pain was no longer an option.

I had good health insurance now and with the help of a caring chiropractor, I discovered I had a ruptured disc in the lumbar spine. It was so squished and torn, the nucleus had oozed out and was pressing on the sciatic nerve. Every time I did a backbend in yoga and had to use superpowers of sheer will to get up, I was squishing a little more juice out of my disc.

⚘

WHEN I WAS SEVENTEEN, I went on a ten-day horse-riding trek in the south of France. It was the late summer transhumance, taking the horses to their winter pastures. Ten days riding the mares while the foals trotted along. No cars, no roads, eating ratatouille made with veggies fresh from the morning market and local goat cheese by the campfire. Once, the cook even made profiteroles, whipping the cream manually with her formidable arms. My butt was raw but I was in heaven.

Halfway through the trip, we came upon a wide field bordering a lake. Instead of staying in a file as we mostly did, we all sided up for a gallop. You could feel the horses' excitement—everyone's excitement—in the open space. When the leader gave the signal we all went wild. I was a solid rider but my giant horse cared only for her fun at that point and gave a powerful, sudden kick. I'd been lifted on the stirrups but stayed too rigid in the knees and my butt slammed into the saddle. A 10,000-volt shock ran up my spine. My breathing stopped. I almost fainted. My upper body went limp on the mare's neck while my hands reflexively grabbed her mane. My body remembered the years on Boogie's back—it knew what to do. It hung on until the leader yelled at us to take control of our horses. Somehow, the mare came to a stop. I couldn't think, or feel anything.

When I dismounted and my feet touched the ground, I gasped. Someone was ramming a medieval sword straight from my sacrum to my neck. I wanted to collapse at the horse's hoofs so bad. But manners had been inculcated in me. Mind over matter! Grit your teeth. Do not inconvenience others with your problems. I didn't say a thing.

I don't know how I got back on the horse. I do remember that for the remainder of the trip, it took me forty-five minutes to emerge from the tent. And that every normal activity after that —sitting, getting on horseback, riding—required enormous effort.

At home I told my dad that my back hurt. He offered to give me a massage. He said with a hint of surprise and an odd smile that I had a beautiful womanly back. I didn't mention the pain again. Nor did he ever inquire.

The family doctor asked me to bend forward, and because I am flexible and can touch my toes even when my lower back is insulting me in multiple languages, he said I was fine.

And so I carried my hefty pain buddy on my back for a decade before discovering the cause. Or at least the physical cause. I iced twice a day until my skin was bright red and numb. I paid a movement therapist to teach me how to move and exercise my back gently. I bought magic balls and pillows and neck rests claiming to eliminate back pain. I sat on an exercise ball instead of a chair at the office.

But I continued to move with and through pain. That was the only normalcy I knew.

⚘

Maman had been diagnosed with breast cancer at age thirty-two, when she was pregnant with me. My first memory of her—my first memory of anything—is watching her come down a large staircase. I pieced it together later to understand that it was the hospital's grand staircase, most likely after the radical mastectomy she underwent in '76. I was two years old.

I remember sitting on her lap in bed. She is naked, and I am tracing with my tiny fingers the smooth white ladder of the scar that crosses out the right side of her chest, where a breast used to be.

We head for the bath. I am walking right behind her. My head isn't much higher than her derriere, and she isn't tall, so I must be pretty young. The image of her bum freezes in my child's mind—there is something in her flesh that has captured my attention. It said: ill. I feel it in my own flesh.

I knew in that instant something was wrong with her body.

When doctors asked me, what is your level of pain from 1

to 10, 10 being the most pain you can imagine, this is the baseline that I measured everything in my life against. I am twelve years old. The cancer has metastasized. I am at Maman's bedside. She is pleading with me to run downstairs and beg Granny to administer a morphine shot. Granny will know how to do that. She had cattle on the estate in Normandy.

I fly downstairs. *Granny, s'il te plaît!* Please hurry upstairs. I run back to Maman. Her naked body is writhing on the sheets.

I am irritated with my grandmother whose eighty years and collapsed arches are allowing her to shuffle only one step up at a time. But I see her face, eyes and lips turned downward, a deep frown in the midst of her soft wrinkles, and I go numb.

She makes it to the side of the bed. Clumsily takes a hold of the needle and vial. I watch as she inserts the needle in the top of the bottle. Extracts the morphine. Shakes the needle.

"*Granny, s'il vous plaît! Depêchez-vous!*" Maman lets out the harshest words she's ever spoken to her mother-in-law. Granny, please, hurry up.

My Granny bends over and rather deftly jabs the needle into Maman's cheek. In a few moments, I see her body calm down and relax.

"*Merci, merci,*" she tells my grandma, and: "*Pardon, j'etais impatiente.*"

She apologizes for her impatient outburst.

So when doctors present me with the 1 to 10 scale, naturally, I say three or four. Maybe five on a bad day, if I really want them to feel sorry for me.

After a year in Los Angeles something opened up in my brain. It was almost like a physical "pop"—a surge of something new. I felt more relaxed, more alive. The fact that I was settled, employed, and had a social life helped. But also, I am sure of it, the California sunlight. I found moments of delight. Simple happiness was a surprise. Our plain, carpeted one-bedroom provided me with much comfort and reassurance.

One afternoon, alone in the apartment, I felt compelled to sit in a pool of sun at the foot of the bed. It was as if a heavenly finger had pointed down to that spot. I crossed my legs and closed my eyes. Peace washed over me. Suddenly I saw myself sitting atop a mountain. The view was glorious. Peaks after peaks and limitless blue sky. And I felt my mother's presence. And then . . . a caress. A warm, soft sensation that reminded me exactly of what she used to do: gliding the back of her hand gently on my cheek, pouring all her love into that touch. Tears streamed down my face. I was overwhelmed with gratitude for feeling her. For knowing she was with me.

I loved L.A. and I loved my life and there was enough good in the relationship to gloss over the less important parts. But two years into this marriage, I received an email from New Zealand. The name in my inbox almost caused me to faint. My heart began its crazy jig again. Mike was trying to get a movie made and, of course, he would be coming to Los Angeles.

Of all the gin joints, in all the towns, in all the world . . . he walks into mine.

I told my husband about this old friend coming for a visit. I don't remember how much I told him exactly about this old friend. But he seemed cool with it.

Mike was waiting for me in the lobby of my apartment building. I took one glance at his handsome stance, feet planted apart, standing stall, shoulders and pec muscles tightening his shirt, and his beaming smile, and I fell into his arms. Four years since I'd last seen him, and the chemistry was exactly as it had been, springing forth unaltered from the dark depths where I thought I'd buried it for good. Our embrace sent warm electrical currents through my entire—I realized then—frozen body.

It scared the crap out of me.

I had a really good thing going with my L.A. life and this second husband and I was. NOT. Going to fuck it up. Mike took me for a drive. I kept pounding the word friend like I could stamp it with a burning iron onto our relationship. I pretended to get mad when he tried to put his hand on my knee, trying to rev up anger as a shield. How dare he show up now and try to mess up my perfect life?

That night we shared memories, a simple dinner, and went for a drive. Nothing more. I went back to fucking therapy. Clearly, there was something wrong with me, and I was determined to uproot it. To be good. Iron will had gotten me through one or two physical attractions already—I would be faithful if it killed me.

Back in my perfect life, the relationship was increasingly stale. No amount of love and fun from family members are going to help in the bedroom, though not for want of trying! My beloved stepmom-in-law had discovered through a heart-to-heart chat with the girls in the family that none of us was getting enough penis. We'd all read *The Atlantic* article on the epidemic of the sexless marriage in America...

So she organized a spa day in her giant Laguna Beach home. She plotted for each of the three couples to make time for each other. There would be soaking in the tub, sauna, a massage table ... she eagerly awaited the results and jumped for joy on hearing that yes, two of the three couples had had sex that day.

That day.

In other areas of my life I was growing fast. The stability of a normal life was allowing me to dive deep in therapy, looking back at my history and blasting through emotional door after door.

There was a lot for me to unpack in those peaceful late twenties in L.A. I was grateful for the comfort and the support that life with this husband afforded me.

With the help of my therapist, I began to grieve the death of my mother. We had been a fiercely secular family with no spiritual guidance whatsoever, and my sister and I were left to our own devices. I was twelve when she died and remember clearly thinking, "Oh well, moving on. Maman was sick so it's the best thing. And I have my dad and we're really close so, that's all I need."

We also explored Chantal's role during my adolescence, and the presence of her baby boy, who was born exactly two months after my mother's death, and whom I only understood to be my half-brother when I turned fifteen. Yeah, I'm a little thick that way. Those teen years had been a dark blur, dodging the angry and jealous postpartum stepmom, my dad checking out of his daughters' lives in order to placate her, some occasional physical violence, and mostly a continuous subcurrent of emotional stress.

I was learning to "mother" my little one—whose own mama had been unavailable because she was ill the first twelve years of her life. I was beginning to understand how my mother dying and leaving me in the claws of a wicked woman caused a deep fear of abandonment . . . and how that could impact my choice of men.

I was delving into my father's many betrayals of my mother, the weird threesome he had set up in our house with Chantal, who'd been known forever to my sister and me as *l'amie de Maman*. Mom's friend. And the obvious growth of her belly in the last few months of my mother's life while her body was eaten up by cancer.

I was also dealing with the rage at my mother's family's disappearance from our lives after my mother's death. They, too, had abandoned me. Aunt Bathilde fiercely hated my dad and his mistress, blaming them for her sister's death, insinuating they had been the cause of her cancer.

I was doing a lot of deep work, besides growing professionally with the Natural Resources Defense Council. My job had morphed from paralegal to environmental advocate. I was deepening my knowledge of green building and becoming the public interface of our pioneering LEED-rated building in Santa Monica. I was passionate about my work and I was proud. I was doing well.

My husband, however, was stagnating. Sound familiar? All that had been charming about him—his multi-passions, his curiosity, his capacity to apply himself with full focus to anything—became his worst traits. He could not focus on any one thing. I'd heard it all—he was going to be, in no particular order: a doctor, a rock star, a human-rights lawyer, an actor, an entrepreneur.

For a while I was the one supporting him. I brushed away the eerie reminder of my time in New Zealand, supporting a man on his own turf while he "figured himself out."

The conversations about life that I had loved at twenty-four, -five, -six, were now platitudinous. Once again I found myself rapidly expanding while the man in my life was bogged down. Claire suggested I was "castrating." Because I was so good at taking charge of everything, it left no room for men to be men. Hmm. So it was my fault they were unable to move forward with their lives?

At some point, Scott took on a ridiculous administrative job in a dark little university office where he was driving himself crazy with boredom. He started taking acting lessons that consumed him—and many a late evening. One night he didn't even come home. I was beside myself with panic. Partly imagining him crashed on the side of the road. Partly knowing he was rehearsing lines with a woman from class he'd told me about.

My calls to his phone remained unanswered. Hours passed. Somehow, I remembered seeing the crumpled piece of paper with her number on his desk. I called the number. She picked up—her voice instantly told me she knew something was off. I was humiliated to be the one calling. She passed him the phone right away.

"Scott? What are you doing? Why are you not answering your cell phone? It's two in the morning! I was so worried!"

"I don't have to tell you anything. I don't have to answer my phone if I don't want to. I'll get home when I'm ready."

He came back at 6 a.m.

The coldness in his voice had burned my insides. It had come out of nowhere. I checked in later with Melba to learn that no, a husband does not spend the night at another woman's house. That, yes, part of the deal in marriage is to inform the other of our whereabouts.

That, evidently, he was effecting sabotage.

For a few days after, there were heated exchanges. He would not own up to any wrongdoing. I didn't know how to move forward. I almost cared less about whether he'd fucked that woman or not—he swore he had not and I actually believed him, which made the whole thing even stranger. Then, why? I cared more about him taking ownership of his misdeed.

In the midst of a lengthy circular discussion, we decide to get some air. I am so angry and bewildered. We are walking side by side and suddenly we stop. He faces me. I feel so much smaller than him. I see him rise above me, puff up his shoulders. He is yelling some things that I am not understanding. I hear cars driving by.

Then I hear a loud male voice along with the zoom of a car: "LEAVE HER ALONE!"

The uncanny support of a stranger boosts me.

I look into Scott's icy blue eyes.

I see a ten-year-old.

Suddenly I am larger, and he is smaller. He does not scare me anymore.

A voice comes from deep in my belly. It says flatly:

"What you did was wrong. I will not talk about this anymore until you can own your part in it."

We walk home and never bring it up again.

I add a few bricks to the fortress I am building around me.

And cement them with a few more drops of contempt.

Contempt and walls are a very corrosive combination for a marriage. Defenses lead to passive aggression.

Which leads to shitty sex.

Or no sex at all.

The sex thing was very vexing and I worked hard to ignore it.

One day, as I was finishing my breakfast alone at the table, I noticed Scott's journal open. I didn't think much of it. We both journaled a lot and I have never, ever read something that wasn't mine to read. But there was something about the orientation of the journal, slightly angled toward my place setting, that kept grabbing the corner of my eye. Blasted be my perfect vision, I could make out a question mark at the end of the last line. Curiosity took over. I allowed myself to read only that one line. It said: "Where am I going, homosexuality?"

My heart stopped. Then pounded. Then seized up again. A thousand bees buzzed in my ears.

Friends of his had commented in the past about his choice

of Adams House at Harvard (something about it being the preferred housing of gay students?), his obsession with working out and wearing white cycling shorts, his two best friends being gay, one of them overtly in love with him and trying to win him over. But I understood little in the world of homosexuality and had swept all that under the rug, reassured by my husband's protestations of being just a modern guy who'd fooled around a bit but knew himself to be straight.

For him to put that question literally under my nose was shattering. I felt betrayed, terrified about the future.

I was leaving for Chicago to renew my work visa that day and didn't see him for a few days. My heart was in my throat the whole time. Scott's aunt hosted me and could see my distress.

"Shelley," I asked that night, dizzy with anguish. "Has Scott ever said anything to you about being gay?"

"Ha!" she demurred with her enigmatic smile and sparkly eyes. "He talked about it. But you know him—he considers everything."

Then she suggested we try a threesome.

And handed me her tattered copy of Scott Peck's *The Road Less Traveled*.

I couldn't quite conjure up the threesome option. What, me and Scott and a gay friend of his? What, exactly, would be my role in that . . . ? So I shelved that idea.

But the book put a balm on my heart and allowed me to re-open my lungs. It also opened up my world. As a way of coping with this current crisis, I decided everything was possible in a loving relationship. The innocent conclusion I drew was: I could love my husband even if he was gay. We would just figure out a different way to be married.

As long as we were married, of course. Because that still seemed the safest thing for me.

I went back to L.A. and buried the whole topic.

And added a few bricks to my fortress.

It was paradoxical. On the one hand I wanted to be loving and flexible. On the other I believed I could only get through life propped up by rigid structures I was building brick by hurt brick.

For instance, I had the "no sex" structure. I'd convinced myself I was frigid. I was not interested in sex, didn't think much about it, judged those who did. It rarely came up between us. I could joke with friends and be open and relaxed about it—but only for others. My blinders were hyperfunctional. Since we were cuddly and Scott would often cozy up to me, I could tell myself that we were intimate. Our bodies knew each other and, as far as I could tell, were comfortable with each other. Only we rarely had sex. In my marriage I had immured myself in my belief that my body did not function sexually.

Until the day the fortress crumbled.

Chapter Eight

Hello Again, Divorce!

*T*here was an email from New Zealand. Mike was coming to L.A. Would I have some time to see him?

That's all it took.

The monstress awoke.

She who doesn't give a shit about anything or anyone, the past or the future. She who decides something in the moment and then goes about getting it with the utmost disregard for rules, expectations, others.

I felt her wake and draw her sword. She slashed effortlessly at the house of cards I'd built for myself. All the lies I'd told myself to coerce my body and spirit into a relationship that kept me profoundly frustrated.

I felt her wake and demand flesh. The lover was on his way and she was going to take him in.

Mike told me where to meet him for lunch. It was a restaurant in a sweet yellow cottage in Santa Monica. Felt like a home. I walked in, my heart's drumming covering all other noises while I weaved between tables to his, then sat in front of him like no time had passed since the first day we had done that in Christchurch, six years before. It was wonderful to look into his eyes without the filter of my shouldn'ts. We were both smiling, possibly idiotically, at each other and at the recognition that there was something between us, something undeniable and quite powerful.

We lingered. I blew off work. We ambled to the boardwalk. I could feel the heat of his body on my side as we walked closely. His hand brushed mine a few times. Then he deliberately took it.

A dam broke. A wild current ran up my spine. Suddenly we were two bodies of water, meeting, ineluctably merging—we would have been incapable of separating, if we'd tried.

I believe we kissed.

I remember being overwhelmed by the complexity of sensations my body was throwing at me moment to moment. The monstress cared nothing for the fortress. She used the surge of current to power her sword and danced wildly on the shattered bricks, each swing shining light onto the lies I'd worked so hard to conceal.

Including the now obvious physiological fact that my body functioned perfectly well, thank you very much. It was ready and willing, determined to go where this current would take it.

That moment on the Santa Monica boardwalk became imprinted in my memory: people milling about; bright, tight fitness wear; roller-blading; exercising; eating . . . and us two, embracing, and me, flooded with a vitality I had convinced myself was out of my reach forever. I surrendered, free of fear for an instant, and in absolute wonder of my body's ability to come alive—an ability I immediately credited Mike for. I was awash with relief. I am alive! Come what may, I am alive!

I somehow made it back to the office and called my husband to tell him that Mike was in town just for one night and that I was meeting him for dinner.

But instead of heading for a restaurant, I went to his hotel.

It was a dramatic L.A. winter night: pitch black by six and monsoon-like rain, vertical sheets of water clearing debris and people off the sidewalks. The monstress was in her element. She ran up to his room wet, wild, utterly out of control.

He got me into the shower with him. We washed each other, reacquainting our bodies. I had forgotten none of the hard shapes of his pecs, his flat stomach, his cock. I would have climbed on it right then but he was pacing me with masculine firmness.

Outside the shower, as he was drying me with a towel, I fell to my knees and, wrapping my whole hand around the base, took his cock deep into my mouth. I was rewarded by a throaty moan.

He picked me up and brought me to the bed, still partially wet. I lay on my back atop the covers. He climbed over me, and with perfect ease slid inside.

I dissolved into another dimension.

Something deep in my throat dislodged. Ravenous hunger, unknown pleasure, and the slapping pain of having missed the feel of him so cruelly. My body jump-started. It's working, I thought, like an untouched rainforest. A perfect ecosystem of moisture, every inch teeming with life.

At that moment I was completely free of back pain, my body open and limber, pussy perfectly lubricated. I was exactly where I was supposed to be, right under his hard body, his mouth locked on mine, moaning.

The phone rang.

"Don't answer," he said.

"I have to—it's Scott."

I flip open the phone with Mike still inside me.

"Hey . . . are you almost done with dinner?"

"No."

"Oh. Because I don't have my keys. I left them in my motorcycle jacket at the office. I'm all alone at the Thai place around the corner. I think they're going to close soon. It's raining like crazy—can you come get me?"

"Yes, of course,"—forced casual voice—"I'll leave right away."

By then I have pulled myself out from under Mike. I am standing looking at the rain, chest collapsing under the force of the scream that I'm not letting out. The monstress bewildered. Why did I pick up the fucking phone? What compulsive sense of responsibility made me wreck this perfect moment of aliveness? I felt deep in my heart that Scott knew what I was doing, that somehow in a moment of Freudian genius he'd decided to take the bus home instead of riding his motorcycle in the rain . . . and happened to forget his house keys.

Mike came to stand behind me. The weight of reality crashed on me straight from the highest peak of my encounter with him. It nearly killed me. I felt simultaneously an awakening and the residue of responsibility to the marriage—or to be more exact, the codependency and need to stay in the marriage for survival. I had to prove I was loyal to my husband, no matter what. It took all I had, and more, to tear myself from the flesh I had almost completely melted into.

I wouldn't see Mike again for years. He seemed to understand, though I was too panicked and disoriented to be able to focus on him. I remember that we hugged. I don't remember his face, or if he said anything. I threw my clothes on and ran out the door engulfed in confusion and misery. In the car my knuckles turned white on the steering wheel.

My little husband was cozily ensconced in a booth at the Thai restaurant. It was not closing and he was in no rush to leave. I sat down. He wanted to chat.

"How was your dinner?"

"Fine. We went to "My Father's Office"—I love how they serve the fries in a little wire cart."

"Sweet. Hey, so lately I've been thinking . . . blah blah blah me me me . . ."

Soggy from the brief run in the rain, I sat across him lifeless, shivering, listening to his latest insight about himself or woe about his life. All the while my soul, my body, my pussy, the unrequited monstress remained in the hotel room, bereft, howling.

Later in bed I curled away from my husband who, I'm pretty sure (like me) pretended to sleep, and I motionlessly and silently received the pummeling blows of a boxing heavyweight in my stomach. The pain was so acute it took everything from me: my ability to move, my breath, my tears. I was a desolate body naked on a bed. I simply couldn't see how I'd rebuild a fortress from there.

I don't remember much after that. I don't remember how I got up the next day or how I went on pretending. I let routine guide me, I suppose. Did I go to work? Did I do what I was asked to?

At some point we moved to an apartment in Venice, a few blocks from the beach. I disliked the dark apartment and the fussy, obsessive compulsion with which my husband furnished it while I was at work. But I had no fight in me. My monstress subdued, I was going through the motions. I kept on getting sick, me who never missed a day of school. One sinus infection after another, the body talking to me, refusing to breathe.

It took a few months after that explosive night for the dust to settle. The debris of my self-deceit was carried away, eventually, by tears and therapy, and I decided I couldn't do it anymore.

Near Independence Day I asked my husband to meet me on the beach after work. I was there early, writing in my journal the true words that flowed freely about the end of our marriage. It was terrifying to contemplate. The inevitable loss of his family, especially. But the alternative, the universe had made it clear, was a form of death. I simply do not have the constitution to live in untruth. To settle for less than Life.

"Hey!"

I look up. "Hey . . . come sit."

How ironic, I felt once more, that the responsibility of ending the relationship fell on me. He'd done plenty of the sabotaging, but again, I would have to be the one saying the words.

"I have something difficult to tell you. Do you mind if I read straight from my journal?"

He smiles kindly.

I start.

It would be years before I encountered the principles of Non-Violent Communication, but I had intuitively put them into practice. Words without accusations or animosity. Just plain, incontestable observations of my feelings and unmet needs.

Nothing about Mike.

I glance at Scott from time to time to meet his gentle myopic blue eyes. He is surprisingly quiet, not interjecting.

". . . and I think it's time for us to separate."

I close my journal. Put it on the sand. Look at him.

Is that relief I see in the way his chest fills with air?

He nods.

DID WE WALK home together after that? I think so.

With the removal of the wife/husband expectations, we functioned as a good team. He took efficient care of the paperwork. We divided the stuff painlessly—most of the suffocating clutter was his. There were no kids, no property.

But there was the money in a joint savings account—money I had received from France and he had promised not to touch. It was ours in the marriage, but only for the purpose of buying a house.

When I went to the bank to open my own account, I discovered he'd tapped into it—$15,000, missing.

I had trusted him blindly with money because money had never been an issue—he spent all of what his parents gave him, on what I don't know, while my nonprofit salary paid the bills.

Fifteen grand! How the hell . . .? And from the cash he'd promised not to touch! My money!

I was going to fight for this.

I'm walking home from the Santa Monica office one afternoon in the early days of our separation and, mustering all my courage, I flip my little phone open and call him.

"I want you to put the money back into the account."

"I didn't touch it!"

"Yes you did, and I'm not going to ask what you did with it, but you put it back."

"You can't tell me what to do!"

"You. Put. The money. Back."

"Well I don't have it."

"I don't care how you do it, but you find that money and put it right back."

I'm starting to yell into the phone. I'm finding a righteous voice deep in my belly that will not back down.

"This is ALL that I have—you know that. You will continue to get money from your family while I have to build a new life entirely on my own. I can't believe you broke your promise. That was the one thing, the ONE thing I was sure I could trust you on. You get me that money."

And I add, "If you don't, I will call your dad."

The money came back.

Shortly after our beach talk, Scott went to spend the weekend in Laguna Beach. He came back in an ugly, boxy, brand-new car right out of a British cartoon. I saw him drive up the street as

I was coming out of the apartment. He pulled up to the curb, smirking like a ten-year-old at the wheel of his new ridiculous wagon, so proud to show me how much his daddy loved him. I allowed the familiar nausea full range. I'd married a child of a man when I was still a child myself. I was a woman now, determined to step fully into my life.

"That" I thought, "is exactly why I'm leaving you."

chapter nine
I Love You So Much...

For as long as I can remember, there was Man in my life.

Dominant, all-important, ever-absorbing man.

Dad.

Boyfriends or boy obsessions before puberty and onwards.

Husband #1 (four years).

Husband #2 (six years).

My entire twenties: married.

Different countries, different cities.

One lover.

And now, terrified and giddy at once: alone, at last!

By now I have a life of my own. I am a full-fledged human with a social security number, a green card, a full-time passion job. Friends.

My coworkers are my friends. The volunteers in the crew I manage are my friends. Helen and Gisela, wiser women in different stages of life, guiding me.

I have a social fabric. A net to catch me. High-caliber, brilliant people who care for me.

I can do this. For a couple months, there is ecstasy. Freedom is going to my head. I have e-man-cipated myself.

Time to play! I am advised—or the "conventional wisdom" suggests. One should always question conventions. Have some fun! (Have some sex.)

But I don't even know how. I refuse to go on dates the American way. It is too contrived. And I do NOT want to "meet someone." I start playing softball on a friend's invitation. We have parties with that friend and her young teammates, and I fall stupidly into bed with one of them. I don't even remember if that was fun. And because I said yes to that one, his buddy feels entitled to make the moves. I fall into bed with that one too. I am surprised, and maybe even flattered, by these young men's attention.

I also don't know to listen to myself. I have no idea what I want, or like. I am thirty years old and, though I haven't been a virgin for a long time, know nothing about sex. Things are happening fast—this guy then the next—and I am supposed to be having fun, aren't I?

But I'm not. I am bewildered. This second man in his mid-twenties seems to like fucking me. We do athletic things in and out of the bedroom, we sweat. I seem to be watching the whole thing from a distance. A couple times the condom stays inside me because, I think, he couldn't keep it hard. The weird thing is, I don't even know if I like him. We do sex a few times. Then, after a softball game, he tells me we are through because his old girlfriend called him up, or something.

And I am devastated.

I call my friend Jasmine, who's followed the whole thing, and run to her place. I sit on her floor with a box of Kleenex and bang the back of my head on the wall.

How can I be in such a state? Neither Jasmine nor I can make sense of it. There were no feelings involved. But the wound of unwantedness is ripped open and suppurating. Something about me giving it to a man just because he asks becomes apparent.

Jasmine is on her couch. I've recovered a little and I'm sitting at the nearby table with a cup of tea. She is talking to me. She is a professor and I definitely sense I am being lectured. I know I need it and I really look up to her, so through the fog of pain I try to pay attention.

"Something something integrity something something."

Integrity.

What is that?

That is new. And foreign.

It's not just about being "honest" or having "moral principles" (my dad always scoffed at that). It's something about wholeness. About being unimpaired, about having internal consistency.

In the midst of this lengthy conversation, Jasmine delivers another gem.

"Your dad was an asshole."

"What? He was unconventional, for sure. But an asshole?"

"Obviously your dad crossed some pretty serious boundaries. My dad would have never made a comment about my breasts. Or my sister's body. Of course that would impact your sense of your own integrity."

Thanks to Jasmine, I am learning that some things are not okay. She seems to have a superior moral compass. Or simply a moral compass, which I appear to be completely deprived of.

After that conversation I begin to see that I have a very difficult time processing emotions directly. I'm a proud captain in a storm, steadfast at the helm, undaunted by the giant waves rocking my boat. But I collapse when the calm returns. It is possible that I couldn't cry about the demise of my second marriage, so I cried disproportionately about a random dude.

I GET OVER that and the summer is over. I am officially separated, divorce papers have been filed, there is no guy in my bed, I can take a breather.

But not for long.

In the fall, I'm hosting a spontaneous party as I love doing.

My girlfriends bring a couple of handsome guys along. The tall skinny Mexican immediately makes the moves. I like his French black friend better but someone else seems to have made claims on him. Besides, this is a pattern I am familiar with: I don't believe I can have the guy I want so I settle for his sidekick.

Okay—I know what you're thinking. When is she gonna learn? I've most definitely figured this out, intellectually. So what gives? What is this compulsion women have to yield, to pair up with a guy when it doesn't even feel right?

Thus I entered another very rapid and devastating man-cycle. I've described this guy as "mishap" or "bad rebound," but the truth is, as catastrophic as the situation ended up being, his presence in my life left me no choice but to do some real deep cleaning.

I allowed myself to be seduced by this Mexican poet wannabe (beware of men who write you poems, they may be more in love with their own poems than with you). Ignorant of common-sense boundaries and starved for attention—read: sex. I ignored all the bright crimson flags littering the way, including my friends' warnings, and let this man weasel his way through my very fragile new independence.

I didn't even like the guy. I felt smothered by his attention. He launched himself against my budding boundaries repeatedly and I was at a loss what to do.

Where was Jasmine, my moral compass? I should have checked in with her at every turn. Was it okay for him to call me at midnight (he didn't have a job, I did) and wake me up for an hour-long conversation? Was it okay for him to show up at my door at 7 a.m.? I didn't like that but . . . he'd brought breakfast, how sweet! Back then, "politeness" was so ingrained in us that we couldn't have turned away such a seemingly sweet gesture for fear of, God forbid, hurting the man's feelings.

And predators know that well.

Little by little, the Weasel started spending the day at my apartment. Then sleeping over. Sex was good, I supposed. It happened every day at first. It was active and changed positions. I thought of it as magazine sex: "Three positions that will drive her wild!"

I do not remember a single orgasm. Or even pleasure. But the form was decent.

Within a few short weeks, his presence became constant. And sex less so. He wrote me a poem in Spanish. I'd always wanted to have a poem written about me—to have someone so smitten by me that they'd actually observe me in detail and write about me. I told myself I was charmed.

His job search was going nowhere. Did I mention he was jobless? (And lived at his mom's?) He had infinite reasons to be disgruntled about everyone and everything. Though his political values had been attractive at first—he was a staunch feminist! A defender of the oppressed!—his rants were not.

When he felt me pull away, he put down his ace card: a story about how he'd been sexually abused in childhood by an older cousin. That's all it took—he'd known how to tug at my heart, that I would feel responsible for him. I couldn't dump him.

I felt my life force draining around him.

Somehow, though, I continued trying to build my new life. I had been working with Jasmine to buy a condo. This was 2005—she'd left academia to work a stint in real estate. She found me a delightful one bedroom in Playa del Rey. I fell in love with the slate floors and wood ceilings, the landscaped grounds, the proximity to the beach. I put in an offer and emailed everyone I knew to send me good juju. I got the place and felt alive and victorious like never before.

Life ought to have been really lovely then. I moved in and had a blast setting up my place. My very own place. With only my stuff in it. Stuff I had desired and chosen and deliberately arranged. It felt so wonderful!

Until the Weasel started stealthily bringing his crap over and I had to find places to put it.

And then I got pregnant.

I was thirty-two. We'd had sex on the anniversary of my mother's death. She'd been diagnosed with breast cancer at thirty-two, while pregnant with me. She was apparently advised to abort but refused, so that I could be here. I don't know what romantic death wish possessed me that day, but I agreed to sex without condom. And sure enough.

I knew I wanted babies. I had confessed it to Dr. Duchesneau:

"I think . . . I think I might . . . want to have a baby . . ."

"But that's wonderful!" she'd exclaimed. "Why are you embarrassed?"

"Women are supposed to want careers here. Not babies! Babies are what you do on the side of your job. Wanting a baby is not . . . professional!"

But I knew I didn't care so deeply about a career. The word even made me bristle. I wanted love. And to make more of it.

Part of the reason I had unraveled my previous marriage was because I knew that Scott, a child of a man, could not be the father of my children. But now, this one?

As soon as the Weasel found out about the pregnancy, he unveiled at a faster pace what the red flags had pointed to: borderline personality disorder, abusive, possibly alcoholic, and a complete financial leech.

I had started reading about the furious pace of cell division, and the awe I felt at what was taking place inside of me was in direct opposition with my external situation. I couldn't understand how something as extraordinary as the very creation of life (Life!) could take a backseat to an unstable man's needs.

He began making more demands. He wanted me to marry him (no). Take his name (no). I had kept Scott's last name because, as I put it to myself, I had no need to revert from one asshole's name to another. So the Weasel would have tantrums:

"You have to change your name!"

"I'm not doing that."

"Your last name is another man's name!"

"It's just a name."

"You are carrying my child! I won't let the mother of my child have another man's name!"

I'd wake up nauseated, unable to eat, dragging myself to the office. I'd come home to his recriminations about something or other. I felt ill, in a constant fog. Any exchange with him left me drained, befuddled.

One night the Weasel and I went to a party. I left early, feeling ill. When he came back in the wee hours and woke me, I said something reproachful. He immediately went to the classic male tool of defensive attack: vociferous protestations of his love, and another round of complaints on the question of my last name.

The most memorable line, which I have hoped for years would be a winning answer to a Facebook post titled "What's the worst declaration of love you've ever received?" was: "I love you so much, I turned down a twenty-one-year-old's offer to suck my dick."

Doesn't everyone know a blowjob from a twenty-one-year-old is the holy grail by which all love should be measured? It was so profoundly crass that it finally seemed to activate some kind of "wait-a-minute" response in my foggy brain.

I was a few short weeks in but my body was, incredibly, already plumping up. The Weasel commented with distaste on the heavier curve of my bottom and in the same breath complained that we weren't having sex. The thought nauseated me. He pursued the question until I was ready to leave for work and promised him, to shut him up, that we'd do it that evening.

As soon as I opened the door on my return, he jumped on me. I pleaded for a moment to take a bath but he was insistent. I was exhausted, just wanted to get it over with. So I got naked and in bed with him. I lay motionless, my head turned to the side so as to avoid his lips on my face. I went cold and numb, then shrunk deep inside myself while he labored above me.

⚭

There was a picnic on the beach with coworkers. I'd just been on the phone with Claire, whose words resonated in my head. "You don't have to do this. It's not too late." I went swimming in the Pacific. The cold jolted me awake. "You don't have to do this." The salt fed me. "It's not too late." The waves washed me. I came out cleansed of his suffocating energy.

My NRDC volunteer and dear friend Helen took me to dinner. "A man like that," her husband Larry said, "he cares nothing about you, or a baby. He just wants to"—curling his fingers ominously—"sink his hooks into you. You will have to abandon your whole life here and run back to France, and even there you may not ever be free of him."

I made one call to Planned Parenthood and am eternally grateful to the team who received me.

And saved my future.

A few days preceding my appointment, I found rage. It fueled me. It made powerful, red-hot sounds come out of my throat and expel the parasite that had burrowed deep in my fragile little home. I discarded-cleansed-tossed, burnt sage and incense and epsom salts. Purified. I was preparing to receive a new life—my own.

Dear Gisela, steadfast, passionate Venezuelan big heart, drove me to and from the appointment. She put me in bed, closed the door, and left.

And then I died.

No doubt this was the right decision for me, my body, my soul, my life. And for the flicker of life that had briefly inhabited me. I am woman. I know. I have never regretted it. But that is not to say that it isn't the hardest thing I have ever done.

There was a hole in my womb. I groped at it with both hands and howled for the absent being I had just begun to sense. I was an utter failure at Life and saw all the ways in which I didn't deserve to partake.

I dragged myself to a drugstore, bought a bunch of sleeping pills, and started taking them randomly. I wanted to sleep so deeply and for so long that I wouldn't remember my name, or anything that was me. That I wouldn't even remember existing.

Weight on my chest. Tapping on my face. Annoying sounds. I drifted upward from the deep, dark abyss to the pawing and meowing of my fat cat. She was hungry, possibly. Or was it that she felt something she didn't like and decided to intervene? To this day I kind of believe it was the latter.

As I climbed back into the light, I was struck by a strange

thought. I call it strange only because it does not belong to my heritage, but it is a universal human experience of courage and affirmation of life. I thought: if Jewish people could come back from the concentration camps and start a new LIFE, then I have nothing to complain about and I have a responsibility to honor their courage by LIVING.

And with that I felt like the phoenix reborn from its ashes. And I determined to:

Love. My. Life.

I set on a path to dig myself. Out of this giant hole of dysfunction and simply: dig who I was. I wasn't so bad, right? I was kind of smart, kind of cute. I could be funny, I loved to dance, I loved my friends and always tried to be supportive.

I ran back to Dr. Duchesneau and pleaded: "I just want to try and love myself—by myself."

Alone, at last.

CHAPTER TEN
The Prince
2005

I went back to work after a few days and proceeded to delve with passion into my new, self-loving life. I filed for a name change, blessed be America that allows you to do that (France doesn't). I decided to take my mother's maiden name because I'd made up my mind to live "double"—her life as well as mine. To be and do everything she hadn't had a chance to. When I got the court order, it felt not like I had taken on a new name but rather that I had shed all others that were never mine in the first place.

I mirthfully taught people how to pronounce my name: it's the Me-Show!

I went to see Fariba the medium.

Fariba's number had been passed around quite a bit amongst my friends, all reporting marvelous interactions with dead loved ones. In a moment of inspiration, I dialed the number and amazingly got an appointment for the next day.

Fariba connected with my maman almost right away. I started bawling.

"Your mom wants to know why you are angry darrrling."

"Because she left me!" I exploded. "She left me here all alone and I keep fucking up and . . ."

Fariba spent two and a half hours with me, answering questions, making me feel perfectly okay with what had happened, telling me my mom loved me and was always with me.

I asked: "What about my dad? Why do I have such a hard time having a relationship with him?"

"Ooof," Fariba exclaimed, "yourr fatherr . . . such a huge ego! Your mather says she is so sorry he did not treat you right. You don't have to try so hard, honey."

Fariba also told me that I had carried these "firebombs" with me, but I was done with that—I'd dropped the last one on the last man. And now I was going to meet a good man (which in spite of feeling good on my own, was still high on the list. How else do you have a family in this society?) Being whole was the end goal. It didn't mean I would stop looking for companionship.

Then she said my mom was laughing because I had always been an impatient child and I was going to get a serious lesson in patience with this man. But he was coming, no fretting about it.

I went about my days reassured and, for the first time in a long time, quite happy. I dove back into work, learning about better, greener ways to build. I met a lot of dedicated environmentalists. We felt hopeful, that we were making great strides. And I hung out with my NRDC colleagues who were also my friends.

And not much time went by. Ugh—I hate to admit it. For all my work of loving my life and liking myself . . . it was only a couple months before I met the man who would occupy me for the next decade.

⸎

MY BESTIE AT the time was a coworker. Anjali was the best kind of attorney, using her passion and sharp legal skills to kick polluters' butts. She was also youthful and high energy and adventurous, and she loved to have fun. We spent a good amount of time together outside of work. So when, as a perk of my job, I was offered tickets to the new Cirque du Soleil show, I naturally invited her.

The show would open in November in San Francisco. We planned to drive up for the weekend and stay at her law school friend Suma's, also Indian/good-guy lawyer. It was shaping up to be a great girls' trip.

Three days before, I had a puzzling dream. Now, I am one to have fantastical dreams. Epic dreams. Mystical dreams. Often really gory dreams, being pursued by monsters that I have to bludgeon to a pulp with a variety of weapons, sometimes in flight. And also dreams about shit (yes, actual poop)—quite a bit of that.

In comparison, this dream seemed insignificant: I am in bed with a man. I am aroused—we are clearly trying to "get it on." Only we can't because we keep getting thwarted by the revolving door of people entering the bedroom and presenting themselves at the foot of the bed. It's very frustrating. After some time I turn to the man (apparently I haven't looked at him before getting into bed with him!). I am surprised to find a very dark-skinned man with large almond eyes.

I bore into those eyes and ask, "Who are you?"

He answers, "I am your husband."

That Friday after work, Anjali and I drove to San Francisco, got stuck in traffic on the Bay Bridge, changed outfits and did hair right where we parked on the street, and made it just in time for the show. Afterwards we met up with Suma at the Beauty Bar in the Mission for drinks and dancing. Later, we piled back into the two-door sedan and headed to Suma's place to crash for the night. We found a royal parking spot right in front of her apartment building. There was a tall, dark Indian man there, fiddling with the lock. The two girls called out to him as they exited the car.

"Hey! Venkat! Foolio!" I was extracting myself out of the back when he turned around with a winsome smile.

I kid you not: it was exactly midnight.

The night of November 11th, at midnight.

Our eyes met in the glow of the streetlight.

I felt a sharp pain in my heart. There was a squeeze, a missed beat. And from above to my right somewhere, I heard a voice. No: I felt it rather, on the right side of my brain. It was a flash but the words, strung out slowly, spelt: Oh-my-God-we-are-going-to-have-beautiful-children-together.

Jasmine recently wrote me that one of my most charming and worst traits is this way that I follow a (mere) feeling as if it were a decree. I bow to it as if it were preordained. No Jasmine, not "as if." I very much feel that I receive directives, and that it is my duty to follow through. That is how I live!

This man was to be the father of my children. There was no question about it. Years later and divorced, I know with absolute certainty that he was the right man to be my sons' dad. I chose well—whether it was a choice or not.

Everything after that unfolded very slowly, but clearly. Venkat was staying at his sister's place because he'd just vacated his apartment. He was moving to London. For two years! It seemed so unfair. I really liked the guy. But the despair was only momentary. Nothing was going to stand in my way.

He was moving to London because, ahem, he had just divorced after making a big mistake not altogether dissimilar from my most recent one. We bonded over that.

He pulled a chair right up to where I was sitting on the couch and his smile never faded. He was charming, if a little drunk. He made me laugh. He invited me on a proper dinner date the next day, to Anjali's dismay—though she couldn't tell me why she forcefully and visibly disapproved. It broke my heart that she couldn't be supportive, but she didn't know I was following a directive and couldn't stop myself.

Three weeks later, Venkat moved to London. We said "I like you" and "let's maybe keep in touch" and left it at that. But I ran back to my therapist's office, knowing this wasn't over, screaming for help. "I don't want to fuck this up! I want to understand why I do the stupid shit I do and not do it again! I want to learn how to be in a relationship!"

She made me update my list of the things I wanted in a partner and promise to stick to it with integrity. (I had written one before, but the part of me that wanted the catastrophe had worked hard to edit and spin it in order to make the Weasel fit.) She also handed me a book with the infuriating title *Getting to I Do*, which turned out to be a treasure trove of advice, not just for an alien to the American dating world, but also to get in touch with my true feminine side.

The long distance was a real blessing. We'd talk on the phone; he was kind and patient and listened to my ramblings and would always add: "And what else is going on?" He would remember my friends' names and their misadventures and inquire about them. It felt so good to have someone so interested in me and the details of my life.

I am at Dr. Duchesneau's office, where I go weekly to run my latest insights or dreams. I share this one with her:

I am running. I am naked and I am running. I am covered in a clear, slippery fluid. I am running through a town and toward a green hill. I try to run up the hill but it is steep and I slip on the grass. With one hand I am also trying to scoop a pasty white liquid out of my mouth—it is gagging me. I manage to get up some way, but I slip again. I am flat on my stomach slipping down. I grab on to a mound of grass. It breaks and I slide down some more. A couple people are sitting a few feet away. They are laughing at me. I start climbing again. I make it to the top of the hill. There is a sweet little home, with a vegetable garden in front. Venkat is inside; I see him at the kitchen window. I feel peace.

"It seems you have been running since you were born," says Dr. Duchesneau, suggesting that the fluid covering my naked body is amniotic.

I had a shot at peace with Venkat. I loved his voice. I was smitten by the story of his heritage, his Dravidian genes, the big dramatic eyes and thick black hair.

He checked all the boxes. He was very smart (a double degree in Economics and Rhetoric from Berkeley that he'd completed early, and a JD). He definitely had the multicultural thing going, having been born of South Indian emigres in the great north of Canada. He didn't really speak another language, which was on my list, but he was exposed to his parents' native Telugu enough that he could get by. We both loved Russian literature, classical (Indian for him) music. Besides having a beautiful family, I saw a future filled with going to concerts and deep conversations about the books we'd read.

He also was on a promising career track, working for a large tech corporation. Though it was clear to me that he wasn't anywhere near what he would become (with me), I saw the potential for the two of us, how we would grow together in power and wealth. How he would use his unique blend of personality, talent, and heritage to heal economic wounds in our society. To be a powerful agent of change, with me at his side.

And how he would be a great dad—loving, attentive, kind. Together, we would create a family of brilliant Global Citizens.

He was a Prince, no doubt. I saw a King in the making.

Occasionally he'd call me in the late afternoon in L.A.—after pub-closing time in London. In his honey-coated voice he'd mumble sweet things about family and kids. Or he would challenge me to go live my life and not wait on him. I was certainly doing the former and trying not to do the latter, but it wasn't working. "You should date!" he'd say.

And to test my commitment to this new, healthy relationship, life sent Mike back my way, just to rattle me. I'd been dating the father of my future children for the better part of a year, though we weren't official with the long distance and all. We hadn't seen each other a lot. But in my heart I knew he was very important. So when my old lover showed up and wanted to hang out, I was wary.

We went on a hike with a buddy of his. Mike asked me to be sure I wouldn't be in any of the pictures. He had a new wife then. Two daughters. I saw the ways in which I was conditioned to acquiesce and go along even when things felt a bit icky, an old program coming back online, running me.

I am walking a short distance behind him, following his path up and down boulders, watching his face when I can. He is older, a preoccupied shadow in his eyes. The energy between us awkward. I force myself along a narrow edge, looking down at the steep rock wall below my feet. Why do I put myself through this? I now see the ways in which this man had not loved me. We had chemistry, yes. We had a bond for sure, an undeniable connection that helped me in strange and difficult ways. But he was never going to be a romantic partner. He would not be by my side, properly, ever.

We went to dinner. I had now known him ten years. We talked about that time in Australia when I waited for him. "Why didn't you come?" I asked.

"I was too scared. I didn't have the guts to go against what everybody said back home, about you, cheating with me and wrecking my marriage."

He chickened out because his peeps thought I was bad news.

"You know," he added, "when I was young I swore to myself I would live a life without regrets. But I failed. Because I regret that—that I didn't come."

I started bawling.

The poor waitress backed away with the dish she was carrying.

"You broke my heart . . ." As I said it, I felt the truth of it. I had never admitted it to myself.

His face dropped. His eyes didn't leave mine. I could see him tear up too. I meant something to him.

"You've never really been there for me. You show up, you wreck what I have, and you fuck off leaving me to deal alone with the aftermath, the dissolutions, the rebuilding."

He is silent.

"Imagine," I continued, "now that you have a daughter, imagine if a guy treated her like you have treated me."

I could see that really hit home.

He took my hand. "I'm so sorry," he said.

I was finally done with that chapter. Among other things, I had learned about love. I now understood that that "thing" with Mike, that had gone on all these years . . . that hadn't been "it." I felt liberated. I could move on, cleanly, with my new life. The real one.

After that, Mike completely vanished.

༄

I was excited about the very real possibility of building a true, good life with a man who loved me and would really be there for me. I was grateful for the time and distance that forced us to get to know each other, and to work on our shit.

When he tried to push me away I would say to him, "I cannot *not* do this." I didn't tell him he was the man Fariba had described to me. That he would "come back from Europe and take me away from L.A." I continued floating with the secret knowledge that he was the father of my children, imagining the two of us in mystical union of Feminine and Masculine, East and West, Eve and Vishnu.

This Prince, I knew, would get down on one knee—and be there for me.

I prepared myself for the eventual move.

CHAPTER ELEVEN

Husband #3: Third Time's the Charm

Two and a half years after we met, my Prince proposed.

There was a lot of magic in those two years. The way we met right before he was off to Europe. The lengthy get-to-know-you calls. How he orchestrated care for me when I was traveling in India by myself and got sick—and then met me in Sri Lanka and booked us into a small luxury hotel on the beach.

Difficulties abounded too. First of all, there was the moving to another continent thing. But I had quickly seen the gift for what it was: both of us big romantics, emotionally ill-equipped, diving head first into inadequate relationships . . . what a gift the Goddess was giving us, allowing us to meet long enough to establish a bond but keeping us far enough apart to continue healing ourselves and to get to know each other without, you know, the "entanglements."

Then there were cultural issues. My then boyfriend's family made it clear they were not happy about me one bit. Granted I wasn't what any good [insert cultural belonging] mom might wish for her perfect son. A French divorcee with no little letters following her name on a business card, and no family you could make any sense of, I was a hard one to evaluate. My mother-in-law-to-be refused to make eye contact with me the first time we met.

But we'd made a commitment to work through difficulties, to grow not in spite of them but because of them. There were enough trips to and from Europe, enough sweet conversations, dinners, outings, to reassure us that we'd make a great couple. The things we didn't know, well, we didn't know, and for the rest we had so much hope!

When the two-year London contract ended and Venkat moved back to San Francisco, I waited impatiently for him to propose. It took a little while. He was scared and didn't want to make a mistake. I nudged him. Maybe I shouldn't have?

We were on our way to visit his parents in San Diego when he took a turn toward Trestles Beach, saying he needed to take a walk to break the two-hour drive. It was so sweet to watch him struggle to keep it casual. We walked for a bit until he identified a nice log to sit on. We'd taken our shoes off and when we sat down I remember noticing them right in front of us. Knowing what was coming, I moved them to the side, to spare him the awkwardness of kneeling on them. I had a hard time refraining from smiling.

He took my hand sweetly and knelt exactly where I'd removed the shoes. There was a rather long speech about how he'd thought really hard about this and the reasons he thought we should be together. I remember noting that he'd really agonized over this decision, when it had been such a slam-dunk for me. And then he said the words: "Will you be my wife?"

He'd wanted to know the answer on the way to San Diego because, having dated for over two years, his parents were getting antsy. His dad would occasionally ask, "So? What are you guys gonna do?" So it was partly to placate his parents that the proposal had occurred then. For me, I was so happy, so sure this was the right thing, that none of the ancillaries mattered.

My mother-in-law-to-be planned a beautiful wedding. I was

briefly vexed to be involved only in the choice of tablecloth colors but hey, I'd moved in with my love in San Francisco by then, she was organizing everything in San Diego, and I wanted her to be happy about her future daughter-in-law (she wasn't).

On the day, I walked on clouds. I was a bride in love and in perfect alignment with her life plans. My groom had wanted to wear a western suit but his mom and I had allied and won that battle. We got him an intricate sherwani for the reception—I was marrying an Indian Prince. This was the true marriage, the one I'd been prepping for. The marriage for no reason other than love (no visa needed). The marriage for family, for children, for life!

I swooned when I saw him in the simple kurta for the religious ceremony. They'd put kohl on his already large, dark eyes and the effect was striking. I was wearing a green and orange silk sari with gold trimmings. I had done my own makeup and made a ridiculous mess of my hair, trying to hold a bun in place with extra spray. But I didn't care. I was struck by how everything had come together, even though the organization had seemed so . . . chaotic.

Venkat's mom had been dogged about the creation of a *mandap*, a platform with a pergola decorated with garlands of fresh flowers. Near me on this altar of sorts was my dear British friend Victoria. When my sister and I were five and seven, she had come to live with us and teach us English. Over the years Victoria and I developed a family-like bond, and she and her husband Ed had agreed to act as my stand-in parents for the religious ceremony. Standing on the *mandap*, waiting for the priest who was late, I was overwhelmed with happiness and a sense of perfection for this moment.

And working hard to repress tears so as not to mess up my mascara.

We spent more than two hours reciting litanies in Sanskrit, Ed doing a stellar job of repeating phonetically what the priest threw at him. Venkat and I walked hand in hand seven times around the fire and threw flower petals at each other. An Indian auntie in the audience would sometimes yell at the priest, waving her hand to point out his mistake. Everyone was smiling, occasionally bursting into laughter.

There is a moment toward the end of the ceremony where a sheet is held between the bride and groom. Traditionally, this is when they would lay eyes on each other for the first time. Venkat and I had known each other for close to three years, and we were already living together. Yet, as the sheet lowered, I felt the power of that "first" eye contact. Venkat was standing tall on the other side, his serious gaze deep in mine. I was bonded to him now no matter what.

CHAPTER TWELVE
Marriage and Children

I was good at being married. Always concerned about the team, the partnership, the "we." I wanted each of us to bring our absolute best to the "we" so that we would create something much bigger than the sum of us two.

We quit contraception and assumed pregnancy would happen fast. It didn't.

There was a whole awkward first year of marriage, getting attuned to each other as husband and wife—and to his family. But I was blindingly positive.

I was also going through an odd transition. I'd quit my job in L.A. to move to San Francisco. I didn't actively look for another job because a) I figured I was going to be a mother really soon, and b) Venkat kept talking about transferring his job to India. It was going to happen in the next couple weeks! Next month! So what was the point of putting down roots here? I was fine with moving to India and having a baby there.

Finding myself yet again in a new city where I didn't know anyone, not having a job as an anchor, redrawing identity, meant there were long days of solitude. I'd been a passionate environmental advocate—now all the things that had roused me seemed not irrelevant, but just not . . . mine. I felt anxious and unsettled most of the time and put it down to figuring out, yet again, a new life.

I signed up for a six-month yoga teacher training program. If we had to move before that, it wouldn't be a big deal. The experience was intense. My body was easily exhausted, though I was beginning to experience pain-free days. Sometimes two or three in a row. It was strange to move through the world that way. I could see how one could accomplish much more than I had. I was developing a whole new awareness of my body and its abilities.

Which naturally brought me back to the bedroom. Sex had not been great from the get-go, but I always found excuses. Firstly, there was the long distance. And then I thought, *this is the real love story*. This is not about physical desire. It's about what we are building together, the family, the life.

And I thought once we lived together we'd hit our groove. We could play freely! But our encounters were humorless. There was no banter, innuendos, no sexy talk. My frisky teasing was met with averted eyes and fell flat. More achingly for me, there was no touch. None outside of the sheets, and very little in between.

So he lacked skills—that's fixable. In my absolute dedication to optimism, I decided to treat it as anything one isn't good at: it's just something to learn. There is no shortage of teachings on the subject—it will be so much fun to dive into that together! Venkat remained mostly locked in a mulish silence, which I attributed to his unfamiliarity with the subject. I was blind to how touchy it was for his male ego.

Guess what I did: I bought a book. Perhaps I should have found something with a less intimidating title than *Sex and the Perfect Lover*. It was bright red and had illustrations.

"Ooh," I'd say, "look at that one—we could try that!"

He'd frown. "Wow, that's pretty athletic."

"You know, going to the gym can really help in bed . . ." I'd encourage.

At that point he could barely hold himself in a push-up

above me. He'd collapse with an umph and suffocate me with his weight.

He ignored my suggestion. I lowered my athletic ambitions and took a different tack.

"Did you know that touch has all these physiological benefits? Can I read you a passage from . . . ?"

When I wasn't in a lecture-y mood, I would just go for angry.

"I need a fucking orgasm. And I can't get there in two minutes."

And:

"Did you know that orgasms have all these physiological benefits . . .?"

Angry plus lecture-y.

Didn't really help matters.

But nothing can help when there is refusal of communication, and that is where we landed in the first year of our marriage. His stonewalling was more trouble than it was worth, so I let it go. The book was hidden in a drawer, and we settled into occasional encounters with accidental passable results.

I was beginning to take measure of the impact of his repressive upbringing. Intimacy, touch even, was simply not done, let alone talked about. My Prince—smart, enlightened modern man that he was—had not been raised with openness when it came to expressing love physically. It slowly started to dawn on me that his parents' arranged marriage may have formed the void around his capacity for intimacy. And that in some deep way we were replicating the business-transaction approach in our marriage.

He'd never seen his parents touch, for instance, so he had no idea how to do that. I thought I could easily show him because I love being touched. Sometimes I think I live for it. The awareness was creeping in that I was missing touch cruelly, but my efforts were met with Teflon resistance . . . and as in my two other marriages, I learned to just make do.

We did not move to India. Venkat made a big career move that meant we would stay in San Francisco, and we started looking for a house. That was really my idea. I felt I needed a home base to get pregnant. "It's gonna cost ya a house!" I teased.

We saw Fariba together that fall. She saw the number six, a peekaboo view of the bay, and said we'd move into our new house before the end of the year. My husband couldn't believe it —but we did.

We found number 66 at the top of a hill. From the street window you could catch a wedge of the bay a couple miles away. It wasn't much of a view, but it corresponded eerily with Fariba's description. I fell in love with that house. It opened itself to me and spoke to me. It said, "Here's your bedroom! And here's the baby room on the garden side." There were green tiles in the kitchen and orange in the bathroom (my favorite colors), original oak floors, an open living room made for receiving friends.

We put in an offer. I watched with some distaste my husband falling for the conventional wisdom around low-balling ("2009—it's a buyer's market!") when I thought the house was well priced compared to the general insanity of the San Francisco real estate market. The poor sellers balked and got back to us with a counteroffer near the asking price. An open house was scheduled for the next day and there was no doubt this charming little home would find takers. I looked my husband in the eyes: "No dicking around—we accept. Now." That house was mine.

I put everything I had into that house—the last cents from the sale of my L.A. condo, my time, my energy, my heart. We moved in on December 9, and on January 9 I got pregnant.

We were using fertility strips, though I was getting really good at knowing when I was ovulating. We'd had procreating sex then. A very matter-of-fact, single-purpose act, waving the strip at him and going into the bedroom because hey, it's time. In the spare room, the baby-to-be room, I put my legs up the wall, sacrum resting on a bolster, and sent deep breaths to my womb. I felt fertilization occur—a slight pinch, and I knew I was pregnant.

My first boy was born October 15, 2010. The birth was horrendous. I did a ton of preparation for it:, prenatal yoga and hypnosis and generally keeping very healthy. In fact, we had been so confident in my ability to birth naturally that we'd opted to hire a home-birth midwife. I was delighted at the idea of staying in my lovely home, experiencing the profoundly feminine opening of my body, and welcoming my baby smoothly into my arms.

Nothing, of course, went according to plan. Firstly, the downstairs remodel we had planned to be completed by the birth had just started. The front door had been replaced by plastic sheets. We asked the workers to take a couple days off.

And then my cervix refused to open. "Failure to progress" is the clinical term. I labored for forty hours, first thinking I could do this as my poor husband, unable to help me, would try to feed me a quarter slice of banana that I would throw up. No sleep. When the first serious contractions hit, I thought: "If men had such a muscle, they would brag about it." I lifted two hundred pounds on the squat machine at the gym at some point in my life, and this felt way, way stronger.

Eventually, I got too exhausted . . . and my cervix was still at four centimeters. We transferred to the hospital where, in the exact opposite scenario I'd been led to believe in natural-birth class, I felt embraced and completely taken care of. I surrendered to the care of the nurses and doctors, gratefully took in IVs and pain meds, and agreed to trying Pitocin (a contraction enhancer) while under epidural anesthesia. I got a little sleep. After eight more hours, the cervix check revealed . . . four centimeters. We headed for the surgery room.

Baby S. came out of my cut-up belly with a roar. I couldn't hold him right away because I was still on the operating table, shaking uncontrollably from the anesthesia drug, but his daddy took him on his chest and they bonded. When they brought him to me in the recovery room, he latched onto my nipple and never let go.

He was hungry and put on ounces every day. *Mon cochonnet*, I called him—my piglet. I was bewildered by how much he changed from day to day. My very first parenting lesson hit me on the second or third day at home: *Oh, I have no control. It all happens outside of my control, and I can just run behind and try to adapt.*

I was mesmerized by how beautifully, minute by minute, my baby was unfurling his perfect little body. As for my own, I gave it the littlest attention possible. It was deformed by pregnancy weight, grossly swollen from the surgery and IVs. I quickly stopped taking pain medicine because I didn't want too much of it going to my baby and I figured I could deal with the pain. The smell of the bandages on my C-section scar was nauseating. Moving was difficult, let alone handling a baby. But somehow I did it, because once that baby was in my arms, nothing else mattered. The one thing that worked marvelously was breastfeeding, boobs swelling and gushing milk and baby gulping as if from a firehose. I may have screwed up his birth, but at least I could nourish him. I loved that feeling of abundance, of giving and being received with effortless ease.

But my boy was also colicky, and a poor sleeper. That is, a

poor alone sleeper. On my body he would sleep just fine. But I wouldn't. After the high haze of the first few days, a pernicious fatigue set in that only got worse over months. The noise from the dragged-out downstairs remodel didn't help during the day.

It was impossible to catch up on rest. Dad was doing his best when he wasn't at the office. Cooking was his comfort zone so he always provided me with nourishing stews.

Our fledgling family also ran into some nasty interference from in-laws. In the midst of the most radical hormonal shift a woman can experience (from gestating to breastfeeding), I was suddenly fielding demands from the family, especially the mother and sister, who had set ideas about their access to the baby. I felt incredibly vulnerable and resented that I had to beg Venkat to set boundaries. Confrontation was very challenging for him. It added a lot of stress between us and made me feel profoundly alone.

Isolation was a feeling I was intimately familiar with. It coated my experience of life even in intimate moments. But alone as a new mother was a whole other level. I had read in *The Female Brain* that women need women. Our nervous systems need to bathe in the oxytocin produced by sisters and mothers and aunts and grandmas together. The lack of it is experienced as actual pain and stress by the new mother's brain.

And that pain was very palpable for me. I felt incompetent most of the time. Scared. I was vaguely aware of the dark belief that if I took my eyes off my baby, he would stop breathing.

Which meant I barely breathed.

If I put on earplugs to try to sleep, I would get auditory hallucinations. My heart would race at the thought that I may miss a cue from my baby. I gave up on earplugs.

Which meant I barely slept.

My baby woke up to nurse every two hours. It was eerie

sometimes—to the minute. Around the clock. He didn't take a bottle for months. He didn't take a pacifier, his thumb, or a lovey.

Only me.

I loved being needed—and being able to meet his needs. Or somewhat meet his needs because when he had bouts of colic, there was nothing to do but to hold him and do all kinds of athletic moves to try and soothe him. But I was digging deep into the physical–emotional bank.

Well-meaning people told me he was picking up on my new-mom stress—which didn't help in any way. I needed a mother. I needed women around me. Women who cared for me. Not just to hold my baby and bask in his newborn beauty, but to love me and care for my battered body. To help me with laundry—not to hold my baby while I did the laundry. To make me a cup of tea and hold me.

I had the experience only for a week. When Victoria came, two weeks after the birth, I could for the first time feel the peace of leaving my baby with someone I completely trusted. (I avoided dwelling on the thought that I did not, however, completely trust the dad.) I could relax in her kindness and her care—of me. Sure she loved the baby, which was wonderful to share, but I knew in my cells that Victoria had come for me.

It is a tribute to the immense immeasurable magical Love for baby that we got through it. Not sleeping. Not knowing if I was doing anything right (though the baby was thriving). Fearing constantly. It took me months to begin to trust that his little life could take care of itself.

The first few weeks, months. The first year. Time accelerated.

I was madly in love with my baby boy. I would kiss him at night and whisper to him, "*Bonne nuit, mon univers, mon soleil, ma lune et mes étoiles*" (good night, my universe, my sun, my moon and my stars). He was everything to me, and at the same time I felt eaten up in every way. There was no space for me, no time.

The marriage became a highly functioning childcare unit. Our boy was magical, all engrossing. We were all about him. We'd put him to bed then talk about him and look at photos of him. So gifted, so funny, so handsome. Absolute parental besottedness.

The couple was . . . relegated. Parenthood took over full blast. There was no question of being romantic or doing anything that wasn't baby related.

To the point of me getting jealous. Of my own baby.

Venkat would come home from work and go straight for the baby. I had to ask for eye contact. For a greeting. He seemed to see me only insofar as I was the child's main anchor. I felt I had to train my husband to be a dad as well as a husband.

There was no more question of me finding a job. The calculation was simple: what I would make in a year as a, most likely, employee of a nonprofit, my husband could make in one bonus. As I saw it, I would end up paying to push paper on a desk while another woman raised my baby. I didn't admit to myself that I simply could not bear the thought of being separated from him, especially the first year. Beneath that, I also detected fear and avoided admitting to myself that my confidence in my ability to find a job was plummeting.

I began to look around at the ways in which my new mama friends were forced to make decisions around work and was dismayed at the lack of options. Go back at the six-week mark (six weeks!—have you seen a six-week-old baby?) or get no money. Go back after three months or lose your job. Go back any later and take a huge step back in the career you've worked so hard to build. Go back to work and run around with your electric pump, rushing to drop off babies and be on time, pumping in the least sensuous way possible, possibly while working, with a cold machine making noise and no eye contact. I was awed by the love and devotion of these mamas... and I felt incredibly privileged to have the choice. And just like that I became a full-time stay-at-home mom.

And yet, that also was uncomfortable. I threw myself into it like it was a job. Like I had to prove my worth, earn my keep because, you know, I wasn't making any money. I had regular self-pep talks to try and convince myself that I added value, that I contributed something of worth. It was funny to me how traditional our marriage looked. Fifties traditional, that is—he'd make all the money and I'd take care of everything else in the house.

Venkat was a devoted dad. I was always moved by how diligently he worked for our financial comfort and made time to be present at dinner. He would even cook! Tasty South Indian dal or chicken-barley stew in the pressure cooker (good for milk production). At some point I caught on to the fact that it was way easier for him to be in the kitchen, where utensils do exactly what you ask them to, rather than deal with a crabby evening baby... but I always appreciated his hard work and devotion to the family.

CHAPTER THIRTEEN

Constipation

I talk shit a lot. But now I must actually talk about shit.

I am so sorry about that. I wish it weren't the case. But my life being what it is, I have learned that nothing true can come if we do not talk about our shit. Really look at our shit. Expose it, air it.

Flush it.

I used to have recurring dreams about shit. The scenario would always go something like this: I need to take a dump, but I can't. First, I can't find the bathrooms. When I do, they are absolutely, utterly, and thoroughly revolting. If I'm in a public bathroom, I gag at the sight of every single stall. I have to tiptoe over piss and shit to get close to the toilet, which is typically overflowing with brown water and floating turds, the rim caked with crap. I leave the rest—not much I know—to the imagination.

Needless to say, I am not relieved.

I believe I am cured because in the most recent shit dream, I actually successfully plunged the toilet and cleaned the bowl to a sparkly shine!

But back to shit. It wasn't just dreams I had to deal with. I also had to contend with, well, actual shit.

Early in baby boy's second year, I woke up one morning with the excruciating sensation of having been stabbed in the stomach with a sharp metal object. The pain was so acute it took my breath away, and I had to remain completely motionless for a few minutes until I could find the wherewithal to conquer it.

Mind over matter!

I got up and put the event out of my mind.

But in the days that followed, I began to pay closer attention to the things that were happening, or rather not, with my belly. That part had never worked well so I knew relatively well how to manage it, but I had now entered a whole new territory of belly resistance.

In the ensuing months, I explored a variety of methods, some involving "shoving" either down or up:

- "elimination" diets
- fasting on kale juice
- expensive probiotics
- herbs that make your insides twist and spasm
- glycerin suppositories that only go "so far"
- fiber supplements that you gag on as a gelatinous mass
- contortions on the toilet seat
- massage
- internal massage (can I keep *some* secrets?)

"Nope," my belly would say. "Fuck you, I ain't doing shit."

I bought an enema kit.

Being preoccupied about output puts a damper on enjoying the input. Walking around the world with days (and days) of past meals most definitely weighs down your step.

Things got so bad that I, the anti-hypochondriac, went to see my GP. He was pretty concerned and prescribed an endoscopy. This led to one of the most ridiculous moments of Western medicine I have ever experienced.

They put me under with anesthesia. A doctor I have never seen and never talked to puts a camera down my throat. I wake and spend a dizzy couple days waiting for results. My insurance gets billed a few thousand dollars and then I get a call from the GI doc. He pronounces, "You are very constipated."

Really? Because I thought that's the information I came to you with . . .

"Take some psyllium every day. Call me back when things are moving."

It is hilarious to me now. At the time it was crushing because I was at an impasse. I'd eliminated all conventional options, yet this issue was still weighing me down. The only avenue left was the emotional one, and oh how I did not want to go there again! I'd done so much therapy and I was in a great place in my life. But clearly there was something my belly wanted to say. I had no choice but to listen.

My gifted massage therapist recommended *Unwinding the Belly*. Off I went again, my nose in a book, diligently doing the homework. Gentle breathing. Delicate circles around the navel. "Paw print" touches.

Shortly thereafter Isabelle, my French yoga friend, invited me to a restorative yoga retreat. My baby boy was about to turn two, and for the first time I was to spend three nights and four days away from him. I was exhausted and oh so ready for a break.

Restorative yoga poses steer the body into the rest-and-digest mode where we are designed to operate from, as opposed to the crazed fight-or-flight where most of us spend ninety percent of the time—with catastrophic consequences for our health, and the planet.

The pace of the retreat was very soothing. It was sheer luxury to take care of myself only, follow my own rhythm, meander through the wooded hills of Los Gatos. I was introduced to a new world of California hippieness, sleeping in a yurt, eating incredibly delicious vegan (and fiber-rich) foods, and chatting with strangers while naked in a hot tub. I met one man's balls before I saw his face as he was descending ass first into the tub. "Well," I thought, "this is my new normal."

But it was hard work too. You may not think so if you saw me lying still on the floor, body propped up by multiple pillows. Inside, I felt disturbed and oddly scared. And again the belly resisted full force.

I picked up Marie Howe's *What the Living Do* from the bookshelf and it touched me deeply. I didn't know I was capable of appreciating poetry. Her poem *The Attic* had me actually, full-on, sobbing. Her brother comes to sit by her side after she's slammed her bedroom door on their dad:

> *I don't know if he knows he's building a world where I can one day love a man—he sits there without saying anything.*

It's the last afternoon and I am frustrated that I didn't get my money's worth of peace (and vegan evacuation). We are in the yoga yurt, lying on our backs, and the teacher is guiding us through a visualization, asking us to see ourselves in the middle of a broad open field. I see golden wheat, blue sky. Then we are told to see someone coming to us. Who is it? I see two people. I see my mother, my sweet maman coming to me. She is accompanied by . . . me. A two-year-old pouty me.

We then ask our visitors the question, "What are you here to tell me?"

My two-year-old crosses her arms, stomps her foot, and answers a resounding, "*NON!*"

She runs away. My mother looks on with sadness.

I go blank.

THAT NIGHT I have a dream. I record it this way:

My father, who is now married to Chantal, has been "carrying on" with another woman for the past two years. I am to find this woman and "dismiss" her.

When I meet this woman, I find myself really liking her. She is sweet. Young, brunette, moon-faced. A nice person. After accomplishing my task of breaking up with her on my father's behalf, I am moved to tell her: "By the way, you should know that my father is not a good person." Actually I say, *connard*. Asshole. And: "This is what he did to me."

In the next scene, I am sitting at a bar beside my father, reporting on my taking care of his personal matter. I am casual, poised. Then I turn toward him and look him straight, very deep, in the eyes. And I say flatly, "*Je te hais. Je sais ce que tu m'a fait, et je te hais.*"

I hate you. I know what you did to me, and I hate you.

In the morning I go through the departure motions foggy-brained. I account for the heaviness by the fact of having to reenter regular life, the sadness of leaving good people I bonded with.

I AM BACK HOME. It's a Monday. Venkat left for a business trip and I am alone with my two-year-old. I have something roasting in the oven. I open the oven door to take it out and put my bare hand on the cast-iron handle. My breathing stops—it takes me a moment to process the searing pain.

I go into mind-over-matter mode. The insides of all my fingers are bright red and already blistering, but I must delay wallowing in the pain to take care of my boy first. I call Tiffany up the street—"Can you take him?" Yes, she says, bring him over. I drop off my kiddo. "You're a lifesaver, my dear friend." The tears are coming. "How lucky I am to have you."

My hand is throbbing, the pain getting worse by the second. Now I allow it. I am in the car driving to the pharmacy with one hand, hoping to find relief there. But no—the pharmacist is so sorry, there is nothing he can give me.

Back in the car. I hear a sound—then realize it comes from me. Howls rise up, unstoppable, from the depths of my deep, dark, stuck belly. They burst out of my throat and envelope me, resonating deafeningly in the confined space of the car.

I leave my body.

I can see me through the driver's window.

I am floating outside, a few feet above. I am watching the howling and for the outside me, it is silent. I observe "Ah—the crying: it is disproportionate to the burn."

I am watching the levee break—the muck pouring out.

At home, the blisters are showing up fully, tumescent and translucent, rather beautiful. I am awed by this body that knows exactly what to do. That knew to keep me safe all these years from potentially devastating knowledge. And had known how to break the final dam.

I surrendered completely to the flood. I had reached the end of denial. I was ready to look at my father's abuse.

CHaPTer FourTeen

Penis

I have a penis.
   It is big.
I am wearing only a t-shirt and the tip of this penis protrudes grotesquely. It is heavy and cumbersome. I put it in my hand, weigh it. The sensation is interesting, familiar. I am embarrassed.

Next I have removed the penis—put it down somewhere. But I know I have to put it back on. (I may actually want to touch it. To play with it.) But for that, I would need to be alone and I can't right now. I am at a family reunion. I climb up the stairs hoping to discreetly escape, find an empty room. But sister follows me. I try to hide the dick under my shirt. Sister finally shuts up and leaves. Now another group shows up. Grandpa, and others. I look for the toilet. Now I am running. Past open doors, crawling down a hidden corridor, trying to hide but no, the family can still see me through the floorboards. Finally, they walk away, and I am alone in the attic. I can reattach the penis. I stick it on my pubic bone, right where my lips part, and observe as the skin closes around its base and voilà, the penis is part of me again and already, it grows. Full erection. Two little girls show up. They might be ghosts. They ask: "What is it you have there?" and I notice with horror that the penis, alien but attached to me, procures me a strange kind of pleasure. I tell the little girls, "You can play with it, you know. You can even put it in your mouth."

☙

I HAD THAT dream more than ten years before the end of denial. Wrote it in my journal. Decided there really was something wrong with me, faulty wiring. I really am loony. Shoved it out of my mind—into the dungeon with all the other disturbing dreams.

But now the dungeon's doors burst open and suddenly: I am NOT crazy!

It all makes fucking sense now!

Relief washes over me as the pieces of the deranged puzzle that has been my life click into place.

OF FUCKING COURSE he was a sexual predator. Narcissist to the nth degree, sociopath, no friends, raised alone on an isolated estate by old parents, sent to boarding school run by nuns . . . yeah, what happened there? . . . left to his own devices at fifteen in a giant Paris apartment . . . nineteen in May of 1968 with barricades and cobblestones flying and explosive ideas of sexual freedom . . . serial adulterer, early twenties when my sister and I were born . . . a self-made youth with no moral compass, deeply ingrained misogyny hiding a profound inability to connect . . .

Teenage dreams of my father making love to me.

Dreams of every single man of authority in my life—teacher, coach, boss—fucking me.

The pain . . . ah yes, the back pain!

Patrick barging into my bedroom when I am sixteen and getting dressed. Staring at my breasts. "You have very beautifully shaped breasts." Pause. "Your mother also did."

Nausea on the beach in Normandy when we are a few feet behind my fourteen-year-old sister. He leans to me, crooked smile, one eye half closed: "She has all the right things in all the right places, hey?"

But also: jealousy. And I say in my fluty twelve-year-old voice, "And me . . .?"

"You?" he shrugs. "You are just a child. You have no shape. What kind of disturbed man would ever want that?"

Right—he is so adamant about that.

Back to the nausea.

Morning at breakfast talking about my middle school girlfriend, mousy little girl he has dreamed about in a white skirt that the wind lifts as she bends to get into the car. And why the fuck would he tell ME that? I don't even like the girl that much.

Evening news, sitting at the kitchen table: "A forty-year-old woman is suing her father for sexually molesting her when she was three years old . . ."

I am thirteen. I barely understand what that means but I hear Patrick. He is towering next to me, his voice seething with indignation. "This woman is totally crazy! That is just nonsense." *Yes*, I think, *if my dad says so then yes, she is crazy.*

He adds, "No one remembers what happens before five years old!"

And in my head I promise myself: *I will never be this crazy forty-year-old woman.*

No one remembers what happens before five years old.

I am the crazy forty-year-old woman.

Chapter Fifteen

Realizations

I sat on the floor and took a mythical breath.

Tears and breath washed me over and over and I realized halfway through the flood that I was crying for relief, and for gratitude.

I am not crazy. I am not unstable fickle irrational hyper-emotional ungrateful or any of the adjectives I have internalized from my dad to judge my own seemingly erratic behavior of bouncing around the world and from man to man. I have had, actually, quite the rational attitude of the survivor. I lived in fight-or-flight all these years, running away from my perpetrator physically and emotionally, putting as much distance as I could and IT ALL MAKES SENSE!

I am so grateful for this extraordinary re-envisioning of my life.

My father hasn't just "crossed some boundaries" as Jasmine had astutely pointed out. He full-on sexually molested me when I was a little girl.

And I survived.

※

I DOVE INTO HEALING. Single-mindedly, radically. A full-time job. I felt such a sense of responsibility toward my boy—toward humanity, in fact. I refused to be a bad actor in society, to let unconscious programs run me and cause harm around me. Ahimsa—the first of the five Yamas of yoga—is to do no harm. In order to do no harm, I had to become conscious of all that made me—including the really nasty stuff that had caused me to make bad decisions in the past and hurt people.

I was going to figure my shit out if it killed me.

※

IMAGINE WALKING AROUND for years with an emotional infected tooth, and then finally you get where the pain is coming from and you yank it out! You scream bloody murder but all you want to say is: thank you.

Thank you.

Healing, I realized, had been my pursuit from the day I left my father's house.

I saw how each husband had helped me on this journey. Husband #1 got me away from father and took me to a beautiful, peaceful, green place where I could begin to rest. New Zealand is where I started yoga, and yoga became the springboard of all my emotional healing and spiritual evolution.

Wendy was an extraordinary teacher who had studied with BKS Iyengar and gave me the best foundations imaginable for my practice. Her studio became the first sanctuary I have ever known and anchored my love and faith in yoga. I'll never forget the first time she guided me through taking a conscious breath.

"The mystics say you are as close as my own breath," I read in Marie Howe's poem *Prayer* years later. I recognized it. Something mystical—that is what I experienced the first time I paid attention to my breath as it passed through my nose.

With husband #2 I began investigating the chronic pains

that plagued me. With his first job we had great health insurance and I was able to access integrative medicine that included visualization techniques. In L.A., Dr. Duchesneau accompanied me in the exploration of many of the surface issues. She, too, became a sanctuary.

By husband #3, I really believed I'd done all the work and was ready to start my life. Turned out, I had just been clearing out debris so that I could access the big fat rock that needed breaking through. And I could do that now because I was in a safe place. I belonged. I was materially settled. I was cared for by a kind man who would support me on the scary journey ahead.

I came to see that each marriage had been exactly right for me, at the time. Each had taught me a lot—and kept me safe.

Safe, mainly, from sex.

THE DAY AFTER I reached the end of denial, I called my husband on his business trip. "I have to tell you about something I discovered," I said. I don't remember the words I used—just that he was kind, warm, receptive. He didn't judge me. He especially didn't ask, "Are you sure?" He listened and said he'd support me in whatever I needed to do to deal with it.

I started with a new therapist twice a week. She led me to Network Care, a healing modality based on chiropractic principles. It's about teaching the nervous system to reorganize itself around new (present) principles. And so much more.

One day during an entrainment (gentle chiropractic adjustment), I am face down on the table. Aidan, wizard practitioner, touches a spot on my back and walks away to another patient. It's early in my healing quest and I am still shaken by the revelation and also . . . part of me doubts. Part of me is scared, still, that I am a little crazy and that just maybe I am making shit up.

And then a breath rises from deep in my belly and I exhale. And in that exhale I detect, and taste, the unmistakable smell of come.

And I am deeply comforted that no, I am not making shit up.

I am two I am three I am four.

I am little. Under your hand I am little. Your hands are big and strong. They can do lots of wonderful things. I watch them build and fix things. And then you toss me in the air and it is such a thrill I giggle and I know that your hands will catch me. They always do. Even when I jump from high up. I love when your hands catch me and you hold me close. I am fearless—you like it when I am fearless. You are proud of me and it feels so good to be liked. (Okay, sometimes I am scared but I push through because it feels so good when you like me.) Sometimes your hand can pin me down and you are so big over me but then it's not you. i know i shouldn't run around without panties. Maman tells me that but why? And then you pin me on my back with one hand and with the other you bring out zizi from your pants but it's different from when you walk around naked. It's much bigger and it's hard and you rub it and your face is all weird. i don't want to see it. You're not even looking at me. You're looking between my legs. i can't move. i want this to be done so we can go play. The warm sticky stuff comes out all over where my pee pee comes out and then you have to wipe me with a tissue as if changing a diaper but i don't wear diapers any more. One time you are holding me on my back and you lick me there like the dogs do to each other (and oh, i have to whisper . . . you can't tell anyone but it felt . . . nice . . . even though i know it's not supposed to. How do i know that? Because you don't want me to tell anyone it's our secret . . . it's between you and me that we do things that sometimes feel nice but nobody else must know).

i am yours—i am yours, right? i am made for you to please you and make you proud? i want to be yours. i want to be wanted. Do you love me? Why won't you love me? Do i have to do that for you to love me? If i do that, then will you love me? Why won't you love me for me?

Did i do something wrong? Is there something wrong with me? Is it my fault Maman is dying? Is it because I came in her tummy? And now she can't do this with you so i have to?

i didn't like it when you put your zizi in my mouth. i cried and gagged when the stuff came. But your hand at the back of my neck is so strong. Did you help me clean up? i scooped it out but the taste . . . the taste was gross and it stayed. i cried. i don't want to do that but i am little and your hand is big and i can't run away because where will i go? Maman is ill. Sometimes she's not home and so i need to stay with you. i need you. Who's going to take care of me? So i stay. That day i didn't want to play afterward.

Venkat is in the kitchen. I am on the other side of the counter and I am angry at him. He's cooking, but he's not doing it right, again. "That's too much salt! And put the fucking lid on—it's splattering everywhere!" I see his neck retract into his shoulders, which round forward. He doesn't answer.

He can't seem to do anything right.

And suddenly I see: that I am angry angry angry all the time. At my husband. I am freaking out because that has happened in the previous marriages: getting angry and finding fault, incessantly, relentlessly, with the man in my life. But now I know this one is the good one, and I really don't want to fuck it up. Leaving is NOT going to be an option this time.

We made an appointment with a couple's therapist named Drew.

At some point, we were spending a grand a month on therapy. I would joke with Venkat that he had the best in-laws because he never had to deal with them. But ironically, we had to deal with their impact on our (intimate) lives, and it cost us a pretty penny! The dream of being in bed with my dark-skinned husband and constantly getting interrupted came back to me. Yup—no wonder we couldn't get it on. There was always a crowd in the room with us.

The good news was, in an odd way, we had a good explanation for our problems in the bedroom. It wasn't love or attraction or even skills, it was all ME! I was the screwed-up one who, having been sexually abused in early childhood, could not feel pleasure, could not reach orgasm, was always shut down.

I achieved a new level of self-speak. My listening muscles were atrophied but as always I found guidance in books. Christiane Northrup's *Women's Bodies, Women's Wisdom*, which led me to Regena Thomashauer's *School of the Womanly Arts*. These wise women had me focus on listening to the innate intelligence of my body, my pussy. I started a journey of discovering what pleasure meant for me.

In therapy I'd cry to see my husband trying. Drew would give us weird somatic exercises. We felt ridiculous but we did it all with total sincerity. Standing some feet away, looking at each other as if seeing each other for the first time. I am looking at this man across from me. His feet. His legs, crotch, chest—and eventually his eyes. Gentle, willing. "Use your hand to ask him to step toward you—and then again to stop when you feel he is close enough." I motion Venkat toward me. He takes one step and my hand goes up to stop him. I am becoming more attuned to the subtle energies of my boundaries—and they don't want him too close, too fast.

Other times we might be lying down, allowing our heads to be held. Or I would punch at pillows Venkat was holding. That felt fucking good.

Every time it seemed to help. We felt closer to each other; there was more trust.

For almost a whole year the little voice told me not to have sex. I don't even know how we got through this. Couple's therapy helped—Drew kept bringing us back into connection and communication. But I felt horribly split, having to choose between what I needed and what my husband needed. Learning to draw those boundaries was awkward. Explaining it, impossible.

Isabelle and I are in her car. I'm venting about my pathetic sex life, but I can't even scratch the surface. Sweetly she gives me some of the conventional wisdom I hear left and right: "You gotta use it or lose it!"

I hear myself lose it: "I can't even SEE a penis, Isabelle! It NAUSEATES me!"

Truth be told, it has always done so. But mind over matter, sex is something I've learned to endure.

That's what you're supposed to do as a woman, isn't it?

ALONG THE WAY I learned that ours was a "Healing Marriage" archetype. It made sense. It also made sense then that sex wasn't the focus between us—though it had been the warning light. I let it go.

I'd ride the high from Drew's office for the next few days, full of hope that we'd broken through, that from this session on, things were going to be different between us.

Meanwhile, we had a good life. A great life by world standards. My husband's job was . . . well, a corporate job with all its frustrations but also great financial rewards. We were good.

And always, besides the deep work, there was domestic life. That job, I was always surprised to note, was very time-consuming. I'd wanted to be a mother with all my heart—not necessarily a secretary/cook/laundress/taxi driver . . . I don't understand how most people (women) manage it on top of having jobs.

But one thing I am good at is organizing, and so I organized my life and that of everyone in the house. When I started going crazy with intellectual deprivation, I got a call from an old friend asking me to join her startup. I embarked on a year and a half of learning and living the life of the Bay Area, meeting new, wonderful people.

We were building a great community of neighbors and friends. Hosting dinner parties, cooking feast-worthy chunks of meat and lavishly serving wine, dance parties for the kids (and the moms), and complete, joyful chaos.

My house was my sanctuary. I loved that house. It held me and all my fears, my tears and screams when I was alone. It welcomed all who came with warmth. Fariba had once said that when the second kid was a toddler, my "energy would change" and we'd move out. I thought she was crazy—I could not imagine for one instant leaving that house.

Besides, the second baby wasn't coming. Baby S was almost three, and I was getting close to forty. So off we went to the IVF clinic. I was in disbelief that we ended up there. We knew we wanted another kid, there was no question. I'd never thought of myself as having fertility issues, but age and, mainly, the fact that we rarely had sex . . .

We were incredibly lucky, and I must apologize to all my sisters who have struggled with IVF. Ours went unimaginably smoothly. We had a first check in early August, and I was impregnated by mid November. Yes, I had bruises on my butt from all the shots, and I felt nauseous and all that but, overall, easy.

The startup floundered and by then I was ready to focus on

being pregnant again—but it was really hard. All vital signs from doctor's visits were fine, but I got, again, really heavy really fast. And full of water. Which I told myself was wonderful for my baby. At my "AMA" (the lovely acronym used for pregnancies at my advanced maternal age), the ultrasound technician was impressed with the quantity of fluid in my womb. I loved that my body could provide the spaciousness and life-sustaining waters so generously to my baby. But for me, it was hardship. I stayed active—swimming, yoga, walking. But waddling up the steep hill was, besides slow and comical, really challenging.

I failed, again, at delivering my baby naturally. This remains a deep wound for me. I so wanted to experience the instinctive opening of my body, the cooperative work between baby and mother, receiving my new little boy in my arms. But again, in exactly the same scenario as for my firstborn: failure to progress.

My cervix refused to open. Four centimeters, again. Dedicated stubbornness. I'd believed that with the doctors' help, the safety of the hospital, Pitocin, etc . . . but nothing doing. "Inept" contractions apparently—though my belly felt like a truck was running over it each time, it wasn't enough to pull open the cervix.

By now I had another good explanation. I'd read in Ina May Gaskin's *Guide to Childbirth* that the cervix is a sphincter, therefore subject to both voluntary and involuntary physiological responses. We need to feel safe for our sphincters to open. Try to pee with a bunch of people looking at you, she said, and see if you can!

I realized that even when outside circumstances looked perfect, I lived in fear, my insides vibrating in something akin to permanent stage fright for something as mundane as being a few minutes late or getting close to a bill deadline.

I can't back this up scientifically, of course—but I know this:

my cervix would not open because I was sexually abused in childhood.

No matter how much I tried to control my external environment and set it up for apparent ease and apparent pleasure and apparent safety—inside, I was committed to fear. And that fear showed up at my boys' births. It is not safe, my body said. I cannot relax enough to open. I must run from the tiger.

I had another C-section. I am so grateful for the safe delivery of my baby—but it was butchery on my body. Four doctors hacking at the scar tissue from the previous C-section for forty-five minutes, feeling my entrails tugged and pulled out of me in spite of the anesthesia, swollen for days from drugs and fluids.

And the recovery is brutal—all the more so that you have to be functional right away, having to care for a new little life . . . and his big brother.

Baby T was born on August 10, 2014, at exactly 21:21 p.m. I woke up from the surgery to an extraordinary supermoon right outside the window, and the nurse handed me my new baby. I was dizzy and my body was sore and I was utterly ecstatic to hold him. This time, I knew exactly what to do. I lowered the sheet to expose my breast and placed him softly against me. With absolute ease and trust he latched onto the nipple and we sank together under the warm blanket of unconditional love.

CHAPTER SIXTEEN

Healing

A week before baby T was born, I finished working with *The Artist's Way*. I'd wanted to be a writer since I was sixteen, but everything else always got in the way. Julia Cameron's book helped me blast through all the negative conditioning, the "wet blankets" and the "crazy-makers" who prevent you from pursuing your heart's calling. The times Dad said that I couldn't possibly make a living out of writing. The time Venkat said, early in our dating after I had confessed to him shyly that I might, maybe, one day, want to write: "Are you any good at it? Can you make money?"

In the fall of 2015, when Baby T was over a year old and we got tired of being dumped by part-time local nannies, we hired a French au pair. This was a great move in many ways. I loved having Valentine in the house; with another woman present, there was a seamlessness to domestic life—relief from chores, especially the child minding. At breakfast, where I was often alone with the boys, it was nice to catch up on the night and the micro-details of the baby's day. Sometimes I thought, *Huh, that is what it's like, having a wife.* Someone else takes care of the boring stuff, and there is companionship.

I did wonder if I should say something about the shortness of the shorts she wore. I decided not to, because when I dug in I found no worthwhile reason on my part. Jealousy and wielding power are not worthwhile reasons. *Let her enjoy it,* I thought. Just because I didn't when I was her age doesn't mean she shouldn't. Her bottom was impeccably round and bouncy. I enjoyed it. Venkat enjoyed it. In fact, the whole neighborhood enjoyed it—*so let there be joy!* I thought.

But the real reason to have Valentine was that, thanks to completing *The Artist's Way*, I was ready to write! With the freedom afforded by Valentine, I joined the Shut Up and Write Meetup at Borderlands Cafe and practiced writing short stories. Erotic short stories.

I'd been told repeatedly that "the brain is the biggest erogenous zone in the body" and that if I wanted to ignite a spark, I should try reading erotica.

I tried.

I got more enraged.

The stuff I found (with apologies to the talented, feminist erotica writers I now know) followed ancient scripts of dominance and power plays that triggered me. I started writing because I wanted to rewire what I perceived to be a severed neuroconnection between my brain and my pussy. Maybe I could, in my own writing, avoid the trauma triggers and find the safe spot that would allow me to feel arousal. In the process, I found I was really exploring the question of what it would be like for a woman to be truly sexually free.

What would that world look like, if she never had to worry about safety, about pleasing, about looking, moving, sounding a certain way? What would society look like if a woman didn't feel judged for her sexual choices? If she could really take the time to feel herself?

Turns out, I'm really bad at writing erotic stuff. It bores me, actually. I much prefer the real thing now. But this practice yielded two amazing outcomes: first, what I thought was a short story about sex priestesses in a future unified government under threat morphed itself forcefully into a whole novel. That novel took a backseat to domestic upheaval, and to this very memoir—but it is alive and brewing and coming to a bookstore near you, if you can still find one in your city. At some point.

The second thing this writing exercise brought forth was my Goddess tribe. I'd met Melissa through Network Care. A stunning, highly accomplished pediatric hospice nurse, she magnetized into existence our club of five women hungry to unleash and go BIG. In 2015 we had our first gathering in the hip Hillside Supper Club at the foot of Bernal Hill. Melissa had said, "Come dressed as a Goddess." I didn't have any Goddess wear—I didn't even know what that meant. I put on a cute dress with Japanese geisha print and walked down the hill.

At the table was raven-haired Melissa in a fashionable, short flowy black dress. I met her striking, longtime friend Heather, the magician mapper of business success. And Chelsea, yogini, model, style-maven, whose perfect Barbie physique triggered all my white-woman, pudgy-mama insecurities. Then out the bay window we watched as a black Uber car stopped, and out emerged . . . Nina. Now Nina knows Goddess wear. *What is that?* A black jumpsuit, I think, but the side of the leg is cut all the way up to, ahem . . . the waist? And the neckline is cut all the way down to . . . well, that would be the belly button. I'm pretty sure the whole restaurant turned around. No insecurities there because of the sheer magnitude of difference between me and this otherworldly creature-of-a-thousand-perfect-curves.

We bonded. We were at the beginning. Melissa was launching her online platform of yoga and meditation. Heather was moving to Shanghai but would grow her women's consulting business. Nina is a powerful soul singer who, with the hashtag #ichooselove, was launching a kickstarter campaign to publish her first album *The Remedy*. Chelsea was fighting cancer with powerful grace, inspiring everyone around her to live a healthy life, and winning.

I would be the sex writer.

We promised to support each other in our quest to be BIG.

※

ABOUT THREE YEARS into this healing journey, I also started working with a life coach. This is how connections happen in my life now:

I'm face down on the chiropractic table, Aidan is working on my back. "Aidan" I say, "I feel stuck. I've done everything I could think of doing to heal, to build a good life. But I feel there is so much more and I can't access it."

"Do you know Kate?" she asks. "She just popped into your field—you need to work with her."

Without question, I got in touch with this Kate, and the moment we met I knew we would work together. We agreed to meet weekly.

We are sitting on the couch, sideways so we can face each other. It's our first official session. I like the casual setup. I like that she comes to my house. I'm blurting out my life story.

"Mom died when I was twelve . . . teenage years were depressed living with the wicked stepmother of fairy tales who couldn't wait to evict me . . . went traveling got married divorced went traveling got married divorced . . . now I'm in a great marriage and I'm working to heal from early childhood sexual abuse. Voilà."

Breath.

"AND what I'm finding is that . . . I feel constrained. Limited. Caged."

"Say more about that."

"I feel that I've created a really, really good life. This is the life a lot of women aspire to. I'm a stay-at-home mom, I have the privilege of being available to my children, my husband. I have an au pair helping me with all the menial tasks of child rearing. And the ultimate luxury: time for myself. And yet. I feel the tug of a whole other life. A powerful undertow that leaves me almost constantly dissatisfied. The structures I've created to support this good life? I think they're now hindering me from accessing my true, greater purpose."

Little did I know that life after Kate would mean the complete dismantling of those structures. Be careful what you wish for.

"You want to take off," she says. "And in order to do that, we gotta dig deep. We're going to revisit the heart of your original wounds. And guess what: that is where we'll find your superpowers."

And here I thought I'd done all the digging that was humanly possible to do.

"First off, you're going to write a letter to your father. You need to tell him that that was not okay."

I HAD WRITTEN many a letter to my father, of course. Not for the purpose of mailing them, only to express what I felt: anger, sadness, rage. But to actually say the words: "That was not okay" . . . that was a first. I had told myself: It happened, it was shitty, but it's behind me. And I would make excuses for him—possibly he, too, had been a victim of abuse in childhood, he had a weird upbringing, he was young, blah blah.

This would be the first time I would stand up for myself, or actually for my two-year-old self, and validate her for feeling what she felt.

I procrastinated for a week. Finally, the night before it was due, the letter came.

When Kate showed up for our appointment, she asked me to read it to her.

What? Read it. *Aloud.*

"But Kate . . . it's not pretty."

She nodded me on.

It started like that:

Dear father,
I must already pause here, because I am already pissed off. I cannot say 'dear' because, are you dear to me? Really? I no longer, ever, want to use habitual words that do not reflect my truth. Right now you certainly are not dear to me. I want nothing to do with you, and I wish I never had anything to do with you. Heck, I wish my mother never had anything to do with you.

It rambled on and on and eventually I got to the point:

That was NOT okay.
None of it. That was not okay, what you did. In fact, it is totally unacceptable. Disgusting, despicable. Criminal, even.
Not. My. Doing.

The writing had been powerful. Reading and being witnessed was a whole other level. I kept glancing up at Kate—she was completely still, but her eyes were welling up, and when I was done, she let tears out and all-out hugged me. I realized I'd never had anyone react so emotionally to my experience.

Not even my husband . . .

I felt different, in my body. To say the words: "That was not my doing." "That was not mine. That was not my fault." Not just to say the words, but to feel their accuracy in my very cells—and that this truth was accepted, validated by another. I was not alone anymore with this—I was garnering power to feed this reality I had long suspected: that that was not okay.

I was physically lighter. My feet barely touched the ground. I had just taken a huge energetic dump. It was all I could do not to rush Kate out the door, because another dump was coming, a real one, unprompted, uncoaxed, my viscera celebrating the event by finally relenting of its own accord.

After that, Kate asked me to read the letter to more people.

I read the letter to my G-Tribe: Nina, Melissa, Heather, Chelsea.

I read the letter to my husband and Drew at our next appointment. They cried. I was moved . . . and also a little puzzled. Venkat had been alongside me on this journey from the get-go, yet it was only now that he was really understanding, he said. Taking measure of the impact of the trauma—like he'd had no idea what we'd been working on all this time. I had waited for his emotional response for so long and felt hurt that it was coming now.

And then Kate asked me to make the letter public. I posted it on Medium and Facebook. I was blown away by the love I received from friends far and wide. The healing was instantaneous. Just like that, poof, that dark weight was gone. It wasn't mine to carry anymore. It had been alchemized by the love of friends, close ones and even distant ones. A miracle.

The sessions with Kate accelerated my transformation. I felt I'd switched to a new fuel source, accessed a deep nuclear reactor. I was functioning on a totally different level. Things that had been so difficult for me and requiring effort were taken care of with ease. I wasn't fighting with myself anymore—or life.

I had a dream around that time:

I am folded up on myself, contracted in a tight ball in the

center of a Roman coliseum. I hear a booming voice from the right side and far above:

"You are much more powerful than you think you are."

And then, same voice, resonating:

"LET THE BEAST OUT."

I begin to uncurl. Wings unfurl. I am a mythical beast [Not a monstress after all?]. I am a dragon. Black. Not menacing. Just . . . powerful. As the wings open they cast a shadow over the coliseum steps. I feel I will keep on spreading and take all the space I need. Then fly.

#MeToo

2016, 2017 . . . I started riding the early wave of our collective scan for all the ways in which we, as a society, have normalized "not okay" behavior. Reviewing a Pandora's box of events in my own life with this new lens of what is objectively "okay" and what isn't.

Not okay: a long list of my dad's comments. About my sister's or my body. About my music teacher's derriere. About women's appearance in general. About how personally offended he was that he'd been aroused when walking behind a woman with a sexy, youthful silhouette, only to find out when she turned that she must have been at least forty. About how my grandma, his mom, should only wear pants and not try to look nice because she was way past being desirable. (So, when you are no longer desirable to a man, you are no longer a woman?)

Women, according to him, fall into two categories. Grossly translated they are either: F, or NF.

Fuckable, or non-fuckable.

The non-fuckable should know it and make themselves invisible. (I spent many years wondering which category I belonged to, and whether I should be visible or not.)

Not okay: comments from other (French) men, who feel entitled to express their opinion about my body, whether what I am wearing is flattering or not, whether it is sexy (sexy always being the end goal when a woman dresses).

And those were just comments.

Not okay: groping in the metro. A teenage girl squeezed amongst a sea of people, not sure whether the hand running up her thigh, or the hard thing pressed into her back, is intentional or accidental, and better not to say anything because, I wouldn't want to embarrass this man. So it's my face that catches fire.

Not okay: groping by men while traveling in India, a white, blonde girl in a sea of dark people, target for hands on breasts, ass, one with probing fingers deep in the seam of my pants. That time I did yell and, amazingly, a group of men surrounded the perpetrator and hit him with the sole of a flip-flop, a gesture which, I learned later, is very dishonoring. That moment was a blip, but it suggested the possibility that perhaps I had been right to complain, that that had not been okay. I was twenty.

Not okay: the man following me on the street until he grabs my ass with a hungry hand. Then in my mid-twenties, I felt a little empowered to yell at him. He just walked away into the crowd. And not okay: nobody intervening. Bovine looks all around, a general, uncaring shrug.

Not okay: the bunch of teen boys, some even younger, harassing me on the platform of the metro. Surrounding me, tentacular hands touching my body all over. And the only man on the platform twenty feet away pretending not to see. When the full metro pulled up, the hands followed me until the doors closed. I remember grabbing a kid by the collar and lifting a fist to punch him until I saw fear in his eyes—his child's eyes. I couldn't do it. Yet again: not okay, that no one in that train intervened, or even asked if I was all right.

It's obvious that there was something wrong with my energetic boundaries. Having been trampled early on, they were porous and men could feel it—especially the not-so-good ones. The good guys . . . I either repelled, or never noticed.

I had no idea of the space I was entitled to claim for myself, for my body. I had no sense that my body was my own and not just an object for men to look at, grab, own. That isn't entirely true: I had an idea, I understood it intellectually and could hold my own in any feminist conversation. But I didn't know the truth of it in my body.

And finally not okay: having sex when clearly. Clearly. I did not want to.

chapter seventeen
The Prince's Shadow

My husband and I were able to have sex now, with some regularity. It still wasn't much fun, or pleasurable, but at least I felt I was able to do that for him. He deserved it. But it was like . . . a transaction. We were waiting for the spark to ignite, still hoping.

Meanwhile the "not okay" scan continued, and something ugly was brewing. I could feel tension rising—and anger too, my dear old friend, always such helpful fuel. Until it had to come out.

I'm lying in bed, on my side, my back to Venkat. Images of the night we met, more than eleven years earlier, keep popping up. I've been swatting at them for a while, but they are becoming more insistent. I decide to let them come into focus.

The night we met . . . now I've already described the magic of that night. The heart skipping a beat, hearing the directive we-are-going-to-have-beautiful-children-together from above. We sat in the living room after basic introductions. The two law school friends opened a bottle of wine and were catching up. My husband-to-be pulled up a chair right next to where I was sitting on the couch and started a conventional chat.

At some point he asked me to join him on the balcony for a cigarette. I wanted to—I agreed. I was leaning with my elbows on the rail in the classic smoking-while-looking-at-the-horizon stance. He was talking to me. I turned toward him and found his face right up to mine. Kiss me, he urged.

I was flattered that this man already wanted to kiss me. But it didn't feel right. And I was very worried about judgment from the women inside. I said as much. So he stepped away from the sliding doors and the light, and beckoned me. Come on, he said, kiss me. I didn't know how to say no.

I overrode my intuition to give him what he wanted. Things were happening so fast I couldn't even feel myself. It took me another decade to discover what a slow processor I actually am. How long it takes me to feel accurately into an answer, a sensation, a feeling. Anything rushed and I lose touch with myself. Which had been my experience forever—this world moves so fast.

So with the urgency of his asking—or telling, depending which way you look at it—I did what I thought I was supposed to. I stepped up to him, and we kissed. It was a bad kiss—it came at me mouth open, forceful, incurious about my body's responses.

Inebriated.

A kiss should tell: Is he listening to me? Is he feeling me? He wasn't. Someone else might have walked away—I didn't.

Venkat asked me to join him in his bedroom later. I said no, laughing nervously. Why should I?! He retorted, perhaps thinking he was being funny: "Because I have a big cock."

Another one for the pantheon of bad lines.

Overwhelmed with responses I didn't know how to interpret, I settled on the insidious thought that I should at least check it out.

Sure enough, when everyone was asleep, that thing-that-makes-me-do-things carried me out of the room I was sharing with my girlfriend, and into bed with this man. It was kind of naughty and exciting. I also knew I was not going to have sex—I'd already told him: make out only.

We made out, and made whispered conversation. In the intimate darkness he seemed genuinely interested in me. It was nice to be close to a man's body; it was nice to feel the warmth of skin. It was nice to be listened to.

I told him why I couldn't have sex. I had a traumatic summer. I am not using any contraceptive. I am not ready to receive anything inside.

"I got you, babe," he said.

We kissed.

He got on top of me.

Penetrated me.

Ejaculated.

Pulled out.

Rolled on his back beside me.

I was frozen.

"What was that?" I eventually stuttered into the silence.

"I don't know what that was," he mumbled—and added: "I'm sorry."

He fell asleep. Or pretended to, I don't know.

I went back to my bed.

The cock was average.

I spent two weeks worrying I might be pregnant. I wasn't.

Then I waited for him to call and come visit me.

I did what I always did: I shrugged it off. Made excuses for him. Normalized. I figured—he was drunk. No big deal. No one was hurt. I took responsibility. I was in bed with him after all. We were making out.

I swept the whole thing under the rug. We never talked about it again, until eleven years later when I brought it up in the therapist's office.

By then the scanning had yielded a basket full of "not-okay" in the very intimate folds of my third marriage.

Sitting in Drew's office, I describe the event as I experienced it. Drew is completely silent. I am looking at Venkat only as I speak.

"That," I finish, "was not okay."

Venkat is rubbing his eyes. He sits up. "You're right," he says. "That wasn't right. And I'm sorry. It's always bugged me—that that happened, and we never talked about it."

He continues, almost mumbling like he's on an internal monologue: "It happened once before—a woman had a similar complaint. I've wondered if I have a problem with alcohol and sex together."

Then silence.

Drew steps in: "Evelyne, what do you need from Venkat right now?"

"Acknowledgment. I need to hear that he understands how not okay that thing was, and how it damaged us from the get-go. I need to know that he is sorry for what he did."

Drew turns to Venkat, who resumes: "I get it—that was not okay. And yes, it hurt us. We shouldn't have swept it under the rug for so long. I am so, so sorry. Will you please forgive me?"

I felt elated. I truly thought we were moving past this thing. It was so wonderful to be heard and acknowledged by the person who had done the "thing," and to be able to forgive and love that very person. I thought we had reached a turning point.

But the truth was, we had touched upon the fact that something fundamentally toxic had taken root at the very beginning of our union. And that from then on, my pussy never trusted him.

I trusted Venkat as a caring husband, as a talented man in the world, a provider, solid family and community member, and loving dad. Never as an intimate lover of my body. In all our efforts to play physically, to find pleasure with each other, she was angry. Dry. Irritated. Burning at times. It took a lot, *a lot*, of disassociating and fantasizing for me to be able to reach a kind of localized tension release (now that I know orgasm, I certainly would not call it that) when our bodies mingled.

The thing is, when I shared with girlfriends my concerns (is it okay to run scenarios in your head during sex with your husband?), I only got reinforcement that yes, it was absolutely normal. Ugh—the thought disturbs me so much. Don't get me started on how low our standards are for what is normal in male–female relationships. Yes, apparently, in the small sample that I discreetly polled, it is considered perfectly right to go into your head and have sex with another man while your husband is laboring upon your body.

I intuitively always disliked the idea—it seemed energetically not very different from cheating. Just a matter of degree, but qualitatively not very different. What is the point of being intimate with one body if our whole being is not actually present? Sex was supposed to be about connection. For us it was just one more way to disconnect.

How I interpreted the information I gleaned occasionally from girlfriends or podcasts only contributed to the charade lasting longer. Oh, it's normal that I disassociate when we have sex. That is the way. It is up to me to generate my own arousal (so he can benefit from it?). So much so that I never, until those days, heard how she did NOT want to do this. How she did NOT trust him, and did NOT desire him.

And I forged ahead. I continued to believe that, with that toxic thing acknowledged, and with forgiveness and with the love we had for each other, we could heal and rewrite our whole story.

But the "not okay" scan kept running, and other things showed up. We didn't see it right away, but that's when the whole house of cards of our marriage crumbled.

I often actually complained in the therapist's office: What are we? We are a domestic machine! We are good at taking care of stuff, but what of the romantic glue? What of the seduction? Do you even see me as something else than a caretaker of boys and house? As something else besides a "good wife" and "good mother?"

See all of me! I would beg. Seduce me! Show me you desire me! I wanted to be a whole woman—not *just* mom and wife. The titles stifled me—and my husband's absence of romantic interest enraged me.

There always seemed to be some depth of connection in the therapist's office. We did feel love for one another. How many times did we watch Drew tear up because he was so moved by our genuine efforts to overcome our barriers to trust, and to connect.

But back in the real world, we never practiced what we'd done in session. I would be the only one offering to do an exercise together—and it was never the right time. I resented that. Mistrust had lodged itself on a very deep level and we couldn't shake it.

I've even come to see how my husband never fully trusted me either. How I waited for him to make up his mind and how I made it clear it was time for him to propose and how I always pushed us forward at a pace and in a direction that, at the end of the day, wasn't for him. All this translated sexually of course.

And the "not okay" scan revealed another doozy. I really cannot pinpoint when it started. So much of sex we conceal-hide-deny, don't we? At least the unfortunate ones amongst us who haven't learned to be "sex positive." We can be positive for others, cheering their exploits. And we deceive ourselves about our own sexuality, living it with eyes averted or in a kind of fog.

At some point we had settled into a routine of sex maybe once a month. I was never excited about it—understandably, since it was rarely pleasurable for me, and by that I don't mean just climax. I mean the whole encounter. There was no wordplay during the day. There was no suggestive, or even tender touching leading up to it. Foreplay, our therapist had told us once, starts at the end of one orgasm until the next time you make love. But my husband was simply not into any of that.

We had done some inquiry into his difficulties with touch and intimacy, but it didn't change anything. It was hard not to take it personally. *Must be something about me that makes him withdraw his attention, his touch.*

I'm cooking in the kitchen and he comes up from his office.

"Hi, boys!" He goes straight to my little guys playing on the rug by the couch.

"Hi, Daddy!" Gets a big hug from them.

"What's cooking?" He walks over to the kitchen. Grabs a bag of chips in the pantry. Puts his hand in it. Crunch crunch. Do I ask for a hug?

"Can you put some chips in a bowl so we can all share?"

When I'm told something doesn't work and how to make it work, I do what needs to be done. If I care enough. And I expect the same from my close ones. To watch my husband buck continually at the "work" of touching me hurt deeply. I can't help but interpret it as . . . "He just doesn't care enough."

Often there is music on. I still try to grab him for a dance once in a while, if I'm feeling really upbeat. He has two left feet and the resistance in his body tells me he's just waiting for it to be over. But the boys jump up and down and wiggle their micro-buns wildly, so I get through a few steps before I give up and just go shake with them.

Every intimate encounter was laced with a degree of resentment, even when we genuinely wanted to connect. I am still moved by how much we believed.

And how much we tried. Venkat had finally relented and read one book about how to please a woman first. He'd learned some technique. He did apply himself and for a while there was hope of (very, very slow) progress. But soon we'd fallen into a highly unimaginative formula I'd named in my head "lick-lick dick-dick sleep."

The other formula was the post-party drunken times.

It's one of our many dinner parties—say, a Sunday evening. We're making beef stew. Come on over! The women do ninety percent of the child feeding/cleaning up messes/putting out fights, while the dudes sit at the table enjoying hot food and booze (unless you nudge them). Friends gone, boy(s) asleep, we partially clean up and fall into bed. Venkat snores almost instantly. I stay up, wired from the busyness and the people. It takes me about a half hour of breathing and guided meditation to get myself close to sleep.

At which point Venkat rouses and shimmies close to me, lays a flat hand on a hip or thigh accompanied by a whiskey-exhaled "hey."

When this happened early on, I went along. Hey—he wanted me. We hadn't done it in a while. It would be over (very) soon. So maybe I allowed a habit to settle in. I didn't like it, but I had no frame of reference for it.

Until one night, I just said no. I felt the familiar palm of Venkat's heavy hand on my stomach. "Hey . . ." And from that very belly rose a clear "no."

He heard it . . . and pushed things no further. It was a revelation for me. I could say no! I was entitled to! A smile spread on my lips as I turned away—I could say no, and he would listen!

Only not always. That's what was repeatedly coming up for me during these post-dinner whiskey-induced mounting trials.

"We marry our medicine," says Donnie Epstein, the founder

of Network Care. We marry that which challenges us again and again.

I was challenged to set boundaries. I was struggling to do so.

We talked about it in therapy a number of times. Drew explained: "This is a real trauma trigger for her. With her dad it would have felt something like that—something would come over him, a kind of secondary state similar to being drunk, and he would come on to her and she would just have to disassociate to get through it."

I'm watching Drew with gratitude. Inside I'm yelling: Yes! Yes! Yes! That's it! Thank you!

Venkat is silent.

Drew adds, looking straight at him:

"Don't. Do. It."

But then we'd have another dinner. Generously sprinkled with the obligatory beers (while cooking), then aperitif (bubbles), followed by wine to accompany the meal, and closing with whiskey. And it was like he hadn't heard anything Drew had said. He did it again. Snores followed by heavy paw and erect dick pressed on my side.

My throat closes. Angry thoughts race through my mind. Why would he even fucking try? What was it he didn't understand about what that does to me? What is it about me that doesn't command his respect? Why doesn't he give a shit that I'm trying to fall asleep and I'm not in the least turned on?

By the end it was:

"I'm going to fucking sleep on the couch! Or no—you fucking go."

Thick tongue: "No babe you stay. I'm sorry . . ."

"You can stick your 'sorry' where the sun don't shine! I have truckloads of your fucking sorries. They don't mean shit to me. Don't fucking do it and then don't say sorry."

Part of me wants to launch again into the why-why-why rant. But I'm tired. And he's already silent. I put on my headphones and a YouTube audio track: binaural beats for deep sleep . . . release and let go . . .

When two people live together and have different habits, there will be conflict. Annoyances. Irritation. But often these are logistical things. Surface things. They drive us nuts, but in the grander scheme of a deep love, they are not divorce-worthy. We don't divorce because our partner chews loudly when he eats or never brings flowers though you have made it (repeatedly) clear you would really like that.

My local poll has yielded some really sad data about how men feel entitled to behave in an intimate partnership with a woman. We have compared with good belly laughs some of the habits that we have to get over in order to love our husbands. In no particular order:

- Depositing socks not in, but right next to the laundry basket
- Never refilling the toilet roll
- Declining (stubbornly) to put on a nice shirt
- Epic morning toilet parties (with reading material) while wife runs around getting kids ready. It's amazing what can be accomplished in twenty minutes. Then leaving obvious traces of what just took place in the toilet bowl, for someone else to witness. Or clean, not sure what the exact intent is.
- Refusing to use tissues to blow one's nose because, ya know, the skin under the nose is too delicate.
- Blowing said nose with hands directly into the sink (the kitchen sink!)

- Scratching flaky scalp all over the table followed by genuine surprise when advances are turned down
- Avoiding personal hygiene to the point of the wife having to ask (beg?) for a husband to wash offensively smelling body parts
- Becoming pathetically nonfunctional at the first sign of a cold, headache, or god forbid mild constipation

All kinds of moody behavior is then permitted. Why not? Wives pick up the slack—with our own headaches and stomach cramps.

Venkat refused for years to see an allergy specialist. He spent night after night hacking and coughing from post-nasal drip. And days making revolting snorting sounds, which would make me crawl out of my skin until I had to beg him to please blow his nose. At which point he'd get offended because I was irritated . . . etc. When he finally did see a doctor, it turned out, drumroll! . . . that he had severe allergies and the medication stopped the sniffling.

Overnight.

Years of disturbed sleep. Not to mention the grossness.

I don't get it.

Made me want to join a nunnery or all-female cult where feminine subtlety and sensibility is not constantly disparaged. And everyone acts like an adult. I'm of a mind to start my own . . .

What happened? What is it that makes men in intimate relationships not want to be seen as handsome, seductive partners? Why is the love so taken for granted that it is expected to overcome grossness, slothfulness? Is it supposed to be a testament to the depths of that love? I am in awe of women's capacity to love in spite of it. To be a man loved by a woman: what a privilege.

I spent years redirecting my frustration at "the little things" my husband did that disturbed my well-being. I practiced gratitude intensely, and it did change my world. I made redirecting a sport and got good at it. But the shadow side of it is that I dismissed myself and my needs in the process. Yes, it is annoying that he chews with his mouth open and his elbows on the table, BUT he is a good guy. He is a great provider, a loving dad, kind, etc. . . .

And none of these "little things" would have been divorce-worthy in a marriage where there is a strong chemical bond. The reason most of my women friends stay married is because there is a sense of deep mutual respect . . . and some good fun in the bedroom. Unless they don't leave because of fear, but that's another story.

For our marriage, on top of all the daily challenges of life, the drunk episodes were too profoundly damaging, undermining all our genuine efforts at deep connection in therapy. There was never trust, energetically speaking, between my bio-intelligence and his body. I could never relax. I certainly couldn't orgasm.

There was something so disturbingly incongruent between the good guy I knew to be my husband, the hardworking provider, the man who would accompany me to therapy and support my healing with his hard-earned dollars . . . and the guy in the bedroom. I couldn't wrap my head around it, let alone my heart. I was losing respect. And loving him less.

Chapter Eighteen
The Last Divorce

Work, parenting, therapy . . . always digging, always growing.

For years I had channeled my inner Scarlett O'Hara—there's always tomorrow! I would do one thing at a time. I would move to San Francisco, marry Venkat, show him how to live and love expansively. Every year we moved some big rock together. He made a big career move. We bought a house; went through six months of nightmarish remodel. We had a baby (during the remodel). We dealt with great relational difficulties with his family. He continued his ascension at work. I worked in a startup. I faced trauma head-on. Went through IVF. Another pregnancy, another baby.

They say with children the days are long and the years are short. We were stunned at how time accelerated with the kids in our lives. We'd barely recovered from the birth and it was time to look for schools. The boys were having full-on ridiculous conversations in the backseat of the car and my body was reclaiming its baby-free shape. I was beginning to look at what was next for me. There was still no question of me getting "a job." The financials still didn't make sense, and we liked the labor division. At least that's what we told each other.

Retrospectively, it is shocking to me how much we didn't actually tell each other our truth. Even though we were in therapy. Even though we felt so connected. When we were in the process of separating, my soon-to-be ex came up with a list of things he'd never liked or wanted, and I was shocked to discover how little he'd been into us.

He had wanted me to get a job (though he had repeatedly said that he disliked how unavailable I was when occupied by the startup). He didn't want to buy a house (though the investment proved very beneficial). He didn't want to buy land (though he told everyone how magical it was). He didn't want our boy in private school (though he'd agreed his brief experience in public had been dismal and our sensitive boy needed a special environment). He didn't want to do yoga, or go to Network Care (though he started a Facebook group for our little tribe he seemed to love so much).

He did these things, apparently, for me. And for me only. Things he'd seem so into and so eager to take on. And now, he couldn't wait to get out.

⚘

In January 2017 I found myself in a deep funk. Steeped in pervasive sadness. I think I was grieving my marriage. I remember texting my husband who was on a business trip: "When did you fall in love with me? Did you, ever?" He wrote back: "Yes. The first dinner date on Fillmore, in San Francisco. But I didn't know it at the time."

That was the most romantic thing he'd ever said to me, I realized. And it made me so sad.

In February, Chelsea was hospitalized. She died in March. G-Tribe Chelsea. How does a gorgeous yogini, stylish model, bright young mother get stage IV lung cancer? Like my maman, she was diagnosed at age thirty-two. She fought it with unfathomable grace and beauty, teaching us so much along the way.

Her boy is the same age as my little one. I have an incredible photo of the two of them looking at each other in front of the swimming polar bear on our very last meeting at the San Diego Zoo. Chelsea had been a warrior then, carrying her boy on her back in spite of her collapsing spine, talking clinically about the treatments. She wanted to hang on as long as she could—for her boy. I thought of a little kid growing up without his mama. I thought of my maman, hanging on for the whole twelve years that I knew her. I thought of the mammograms I get diligently each year since I turned thirty-two.

I deluded myself that Chelsea was winning. And she did, in a way—she let go of her body and won her spiritual freedom. She ascended—and elevated those around her.

But her death also shattered my heart. And once the little pieces were floating out there in space, they never came back together the same.

I HAD HUNG on to my third marriage for dear life. I hung on and hung on in the face of repeated evidence. I batted at the doubts gnawing at me with therapy and books and mind-control tricks. I made focusing on good traits a sport, swatting away at criticism like a tennis player on the receiving end of a ball-popping machine. Diligently. Yes, this is annoying but, yes, this doesn't work but, yes, but!

In a last-ditch effort, we even attempted to "open" our marriage. I continued lying to myself. This can work! I can have my cake and eat it too! I can love this kind man, father of my children, we can live harmoniously, raise our kids together, share a household, so sweet. AND we can go visit our lovers once or twice a week.

Needless to say, that didn't go well and delivered the last nail into our marriage coffin. Does it matter, at the end of the day, how we got to the conclusion that we were done for good? Why should it?

One Sunday evening in May, Venkat read me a long letter he'd written. In it, he portrayed himself as the stalwart of our marriage and projected an image that had never even entered the window—romantic togetherness, growing old together, etc. . . . He ended his reading with a question—or perhaps a statement: "For it to work, we have to step back into a conventional marriage."

I stayed silent for a long while, listening for the right words to come up from the depths of me. Or rather the one word.

The silence was absolute and perfect. I had time to feel my breath. I had time to feel and savor, even, the strength of my resolution. I also had time to consider (and resent) the fact that I was once more being pushed into the corner where I would be the one saying it. It pissed me off mildly because having gone through this twice before, I was shocked by how far men (even a good one like this one) would go to avoid being the one saying it. They'd rather hang in a yucky status quo or practice sabotage than say it. They want me to say it because . . . what, then I'm the bad guy? And that makes it better for their ego? Shrug.

The word came eventually. It came simply and without any of the drama you might imagine. The drama had been before. Now was time for deep, unavoidable, unquestionable truth. So: no. No I cannot fit back into this marriage.

I'm sitting in my favorite orange felt swivel chair at the foot of the bed. Venkat is propped up in bed. I have been quiet for a good moment. I am painfully aware that this is serious grown-up shit and I have to dive into it.

Me: "No."

Him: "We separate, then."
Me: "Yes."

A deep breath followed. I had the strangest sensation that a body inside my flesh body had been squeezed in and suddenly, whoosh, burst out of its artificial boundaries and expanded outward in all directions.

There was relief.

chapter nineteen
A New Chapter

I.

Large hand wrapped around my neck.
Firm.
Holding me down.

My eyes follow the veins snaking up the muscular forearm.
Along the flexed bicep.
Up past a sinewy boxer's shoulder.
I lock onto wide irises, blue, boring into mine.
And I moan.
My body—finally!—used, not *ab*used, according to its
(divine)
design.

Pinned—deliciously, into willing surrender.
Succumbed, to the tireless thrust of my lover's hips.
Relaxed, into deep connection.
Receiving him, with trusting abandon.

I'm game. I am game.
I am *his* game.
Prey?

Oh! I prayed for this. Yes, pursue me, chase me and . . .
consume me.
Play! With me.

My whirling tantrum of decades—the rage of frustration,
of my body used in wrong ways while
unseen, unheard, unappreciated,
unsafe.
Rage—finally abating.

Adding my drop of honey into the bloodstream of the Goddess
Doing my bit to calm *Her* Cosmic Tantrum of Centuries
as She called and called
and called
for her Equal to finally, fully,
Show. The Fuck. Up.

I am no longer in fear (and possibly hatred) of men.
I divorced, and divorced, and divorced . . .
and still proceeded to fall in love.

With *me*.

I gathered the disintegrated pieces of my soul,
regained my integrity.
I can *feel* my own boundaries.
And because I now *know* me—
Then, of course, I *love* me.

And because I can love me,
I can *choose*
to open my borders,

to share my Self.
My true self.

And so it is that I can truly love . . . an "other."

Open-hearted love, balls-out love, all-penetrating love.
A love I dove into not because the mind checks boxes but because it *feels* right.
Attuned with the body every instant,
her wisdom informing me.
"Do I want this?" (yes)
"Do I want this?" (yes)
I am finally able to hear her, heed her.

I no longer ignore, or force.
I flow around the barrage of shoulds,
of this-is-how-it's-done and this-is-not-done.
The mirage of externally imposed rules evaporating.

I acquiesce, humbled by the accuracy of her delicate voice,
guiding me now through the great adventure
I always yearned for.
Partnership.

Yes, she said.
Him.

II.

Sisters.
Why have we worked so hard to fit in,
when we could be fireworks?

Each of us exploding with our own unique colors,
unrestrained,
painting a luminous ensemble into the cosmic night?

We were so fearful, little ones,
hanging on to the rail,
not trusting we could fly.
That wild woman inside? Why did she hide?
The wise, or creative, or "simply" loving one? Why did she hide?
"Too much," they'd say, "she will ruin 'society.'
She should *behave* so the wheels can continue grinding."

And our men too,
who were taught that the soft spot inside of them should be—
like anything of the feminine—
ignored, trampled, gagged.

Inside, outside.
Everyone suffered.

Those stories have almost ruined us.
They calcified over our hearts, nearly suffocating us,
along with every other species—even Earth herself.

Seriously, have you *seen* the way we live?
It harms—hurts—pollutes—separates.
Mama Gaia's body unseen, unheard, unappreciated—
her generous gifts consumed mindlessly,
rapidly.

Space and time collapsing,
No room to breathe, to be.

And oh—our body! Manifest creation of the Goddess—
as is everything else, in the universe of form—
we treat it like we treat our Planet.
"Oxygen? Water? Plants? A beating heart?
That is just to be expected!"
Taken for granted.

But the body talks.
Mine screaming at me for decades.
Back-head-belly aches.

I ignored, pushed through, overriding my intuition
(as we were taught),
landing in a neutral territory of mild misery,
wondering daily what was that ennui,
why I simply couldn't be content with the lovely life I'd built.

Because it wasn't true!
It had required trampling the body,
a tamed-down energetic re-enactment of my father's sins.

Recently, my body spoke to me in a Haiku:

> *Can't you see I starve?*
> *I need more food! Freedom! Love!*
> *Why question my needs?*

Why, indeed.

III.

So listen!
And unravel, if you must
(the lies, the shoulds, the old stories).
Dive deep, rise high, Divine Feminine!
Join the Priestess Temples
Find your Grace,
your Sovereignty.
It is sacred and, always,
with(in) you.

Know that You Are Love.
I am love! Love is me! And you! In a body!

That very force that moves planets and gives birth and grows.
Call it Life, Goddess, Shakti, Prana—
it is Love and tag! You're it!

Knowing that, how could you ever be "wrong"?

Love heals all.
Hands on my body, without love, is abuse and trauma.
But *in love*, oh!
Feel the connection, reverence, ecstasy.

Ecstasy: what we should all aim for.
Of wild, unabashed pleasure of the self.
Honoring the body so deeply, so truly,
that it is impossible not to gush with awe
at every moment of this being-alive-in-a-human-body ride.

Nourish Her, praise Her, see Her—
may She feel safe, held, appreciated.
She: the body, the Goddess, the Earth,
the Feminine in all of us . . .

I am one of Her cells, doing my tiny bit. You are too.
She, through us, has only just begun to shake herself awake,
untie all sorts of (marriage) knots, and dance again—
alongside her Equal Partner.

Just you watch, World, with cheer if you may,
as she unfolds Her myriad gifts
and uses the only true power (Love!) to heal, to play,
to joyfully recreate.
Re-create.

acknowledgments

In late spring of 2017 I got a call from my Sister Goddess Christine Hutcheson. She said: "Evelyne! We are watching you go through this divorce with so much grace, you have so much wisdom to share, you should write a book about it and title it 'The Goddess Guide to Divorce'!" She planted the seed and gifted me with her belief in me, her support, and even the title. This book would not be without her. And it would not be what it is without my gifted editor Miranda Culp. Miranda was the Goddess's gift to me and to this book. She waded fiercely through the warm pile of not-so-good writing I sent her, extracted the gems, and proceeded to guide me through the polishing of my first book with the perfect mix of straight-talk and cheer. My awe and thanks are also owed to Stacey Aaronson who instantly "got" this memoir and magically turned it into an actual book with a delightful cover.

I am deeply grateful to Venkat, third husband and father of my two boys, for supporting me steadily through my healing journey and when I decided to launch myself fully into writing, and for showing up as a first-class co-parent since our separation.

Along the entire year that I focused on this memoir, I kept growing and exploring deeper dimensions of the Divine Feminine thanks to my beloved teacher Grace Galzagorry, and to the archetypal work developed by Ariel Spilsbury. This book came fully to life through the unconditional support of my Thirteen Moons Sisters and Brother, which included the exquisite guidance of our focalizer Elana Auerbach. I am eternally grateful for the profound dedication of everyone in these circles to the work of raising our consciousness, and to the One Heart.

With all dimensions of my expanded heart I want to thank Neil for showing up as I was just beginning to write this story. And showing up, day after day, to see me, appreciate me, make love to me.

And finally, of course: my humble gratitude to the Goddess for all the mysterious ways—friends, foes, animate and inanimate, serendipity and seeming setbacks—in which she chose to manifest herself.

> Every beat of my heart
> A thundering THANK YOU
> (thank you, thank you, thank you)
> Can you hear it?
>
> Gratitude on a loop
> no matter what
> for being me.

This book is truly a work of Love. Thank you.

about the author

EVELYNE MICHAUT was born and raised in France, from where she sprung, at nineteen, into a worldwide holy quest for true love, home, and family. She found healing and salvation through writing at an early age, but took her sweet time to believe she could make it a public career.

The Goddess Guide to Divorce is her first (finished) book. With this memoir out of the way, Evelyne will resume work on the first draft of a futuristic feminine novel where Priestesses and the fledgling Unified Planetary Government they helped create are under threat.

While she continues steadily her process of disidentification, Evelyne still cherishes the experiences beneath the labels of mother, lover, and writer. Her life is an ongoing adventure revolving around her magnificent four- and eight-year-old boys, her legendary love, and the stories that are demanding to be written.

www.ingramcontent.com/pod-product-compliance
Lightning Source LLC
Chambersburg PA
CBHW020412080526
44584CB00014B/1295